I0129196

Barrett Wendell

The Duchess Emilia

A Romance

Barrett Wendell

The Duchess Emilia
A Romance

ISBN/EAN: 9783744673662

Printed in Europe, USA, Canada, Australia, Japan

Cover: Foto ©Thomas Meinert / pixelio.de

More available books at **www.hansebooks.com**

THE DUCHESS EMILIA

A ROMANCE

BY

BARRETT WENDELL

> " The soul that rises with us, our life's star,
> Hath had elsewhere its setting."
> WORDSWORTH.

BOSTON
JAMES R. OSGOOD AND COMPANY
1885

Copyright, 1885,
By James R. Osgood and Company.

All rights reserved.

University Press:
John Wilson and Son, Cambridge.

THE DUCHESS EMILIA.

INTRODUCTION.

THE Rome of the Caesars is dead and
gone, — dead and gone like that shadowy
Rome whose secret name lay hidden in the
hearts of her priests. And there is another
Rome, a Rome our fathers knew, a Rome
we saw ourselves, which shall be seen no
more by men. Indeed, it seems now that men
will see less of the Rome of the Popes than
of the older cities on which she reared herself. For scientific people are at work digging
up Forums, and breaking great boulevards
through the heart of the houses, where filth
and fever, and picturesque things speakable
and unspeakable, used to dwell together in
peace under the Holy Fathers' sway. The

stones that were worn by the sandalled feet of consuls and the chariot-wheels of imperial generals are coming to light once more. The streets whose dust blew about the gilded coaches of the Cardinals are vanishing away. The old papal times are a legend to children, — such a legend as British rule was to American children when our Republic was new. And men who love to dream, look back to those times already as to a fantastic past, where in clouds of color and glory things of this world and of the next — sin and holiness, ecstasy and intrigue, beauty and passion, charity and grandeur — rolled inseparably mingled before the eyes alike of those who bowed before the Vicegerent of Christ, and of those who stood erect as he passed.

The tale I wish to tell is a tale of that vanished Rome. The man whose papers tell the tale to me lived in years not far gone. The mill his father built on the Merrimac still pays dividends. And for aught I know the friends he knew in Rome are still in Rome, rejoicing or sorrowing in the rule of hirsute King Humbert. In plain figures, it is not quite forty years since Richard Beverly went to Italy, yet it is long enough for him to have become a strangely mystic figure of the past, who seems as unreal to-day as does the Rome of which his writing tells.

He was my kinsman. To be sure, I never saw him. When I was born he was already dead. When I was old enough to hear his name, he was spoken of as an erratic person, whose unspecified but singular behavior had been by no means what should have been looked for from a respectable American. Our people were men of affairs, who thought more about cotton than about poetry. As for romance or mystery, I doubt that you could have taught them what the words mean.

Perhaps from the fondness for opposition common in children, perhaps — and I like to think so — from some sympathy that would have made me Richard Beverly's friend, had he lived to know me, I grew first to wondering what his singular behavior could have been; then to conjuring up all manner of strange deeds, heroic and mystical, and attributing them to him; finally to loving the kindly and romantic figure which I called by. his name. The delight that some children find in half-believed day-dreams of cities and kingdoms which their fancy builds, I found in dreaming of Richard Beverly. I conjured up a Rome for him to dwell in; I conjured up his figure as the most potent dweller therein. I grew to think of him as mine, and to love him with all the self-applauding intensity of a creator.

Years afterwards — not long ago, in fact — I came across the papers that were sent home from Rome when Beverly died. I read them with an interest perhaps exaggerated by the fantastic memories that in my mind clustered about his name. Yet making all allowance for this prejudice, it seemed to me that his last days, unlike as they were to the grand career that I had been used to dream about as his, had a strange beauty of their own. And this beauty, I thought, might win from others for his memory such loving admiration as it wins from me, — an admiration far different from that which in my childhood I blindly gave to the legends I wove about his name.

So I have made up my mind to tell his story. I shall tell it chiefly in his own words, adding only such passages as are needed to explain them. In so doing I feel that I do tardy justice to one whom those that knew him misjudged. Richard Beverly is remembered by those who remember him at all as a foolish madman. He ought to be so thought of no more. Mad, indeed, he may have been; but their hearts must be harder than mine who do not see something more than folly gleaming through the clouds that closed about his life in the midst of Pope Gregory's Rome, — a Rome now as dead and as forgotten of the world as is Beverly himself.

I.

RICHARD BEVERLY was the only child of parents who married late in life. He came of one of those old New England families that live through generation after generation in country pulpits, until at length the energy that has been gathering in the stock reveals itself, usually in no very ministerial way. Richard's father it was who brought the Beverlys out of the Orthodox Church and into the world. A remarkably keen man of business, he was in early life one of those who founded the great mills that have made the commercial fortune of New England; and in a money way he prospered exceedingly. Richard Beverly left a handsome estate.

Along with fortune came to old Mr. Beverly the curse that the long agonies of our pious fathers have handed down to us, to temper the blessings of their sharp wit and their honesty.

He would fall into fits of despondency so deep that his friends would grow seriously alarmed. At last he was observed to eye his razor with so fond a glance that it was thought well to put him under control for a while. So, not unwillingly, for he was quite aware of his infirmity, he was bundled off to an asylum, where he soon recovered from the attack. This timely proceeding, which undoubtedly saved him from one fate, resulted in plunging him into another. At the asylum was a lady, no longer in the first bloom of youth, whose excessively romantic behavior had led competent authorities to pronounce her mind unbalanced; so she had been temporarily retired from the world. She had known Mr. Beverly of old. His merits, which were mostly of the practical sort, had never appealed to her in general society. But now that the pair were thrown together perforce, she discovered in him many admirable traits. Indeed, I suppose that any susceptible woman is sure to discover them in a man whom she is compelled to see every day. And any susceptible woman may be trusted to do what this one did, namely, to fall very honestly in love with the possessor of the traits in question. Whether Mr. Beverly fell in love with her or not has never been quite settled. However this may have been, they were married, to the great scandal of society, soon after they emerged from the singular place which had witnessed their courtship.

The marriage was a happy one. Mrs. Beverly turned out to be an excellent house-keeper; and as duties began to present themselves she found no more time for romance. So, barring a very marked experience of religion a year or two before she died, she was perfectly sane for the rest of her life. Mr. Beverly was not so lucky. He went on and prospered for some years, and gave good dinners, and bought a good deal of celebrated Madeira. Then, one day, overwork or the strength of Puritan sadness asserting itself in spite of environment, put an end to dinners and Madeira and cotton and clubs. He cut his throat. His was one

of the first of the marble monuments that make
ghastly the hills of Mount Auburn.

That Richard Beverly, coming of such par-
entage, should be a strange fellow was only
to be expected. So much was it to be expected, indeed, that everybody who knew him
was on the watch for oddities; and with that
sage acuteness which people show when their
attention is aroused, his friends were prepared
to assert that they observed something uncanny
even in his baby cries. Yet, after all, so far as
I can discover from what tales of his childhood
remain after sixty years and more, he was in
many respects a normal boy enough. To be
sure, he was self-conscious; but then, he was
the solitary pet of a sentimental woman advanc-
ing in years, and besides, he was very handsome.
A portrait of him is still preserved. It is very
ill-painted. But all that the painter could do
to caricature the boy, who sits in his best green
jacket and broad white collar, stiffly leaning his
head upon his right hand, could not conceal
his marvellous great eyes, and his clean-cut

features, and his rich dark skin, and his bil-
lowy black curls. So, just as Mrs. Beverly
spoiled him because he was her son, other
people must have spoiled him because he was
a beauty.

There is no doubt, too, that he had a curiously sensitive nature and a sense of honor so
fantastic that it sometimes got him into trouble
with his less high-strung acquaintance. Once,
when a cousin of about his own age began, in
a fit of confidence, to tell Richard some child-
ish secret of unspeakable importance for the
moment, Richard begged him to stop. For,
the strange child observed, if somebody should
happen to ask him whether he knew anything
about the matter in question he should have
to answer yes. Upon this declaration of prin-
ciple a fight ensued, in which Richard was
worsted ; and the consequent wrath of his
mother gave rise to a family feud that was
not healed until the assailing cousin came, in
a spirit of Christian condonation, to Mrs. Beverly's funeral. The feud preserved the story.

There is another tale of him when he was a little older, which I have from my mother. At dancing-school, where from time out of mind the youth of Boston have made their first appearance in the social world, she was something of a belle. One day Richard Beverly came running into the room, quite out of breath, and invited her to dance with him. She had hardly accepted when another admirer followed in his footsteps. Whereupon, before she had time to decline the second invitation, Richard grew very red in the face, and stammering a little, amazed her by declaring that he thought she had better dance with the other boy.

" The fact is," he said, " I heard him say that he was going to ask you ; and I ran in first. I don't think I was quite fair."

And thereupon, Master Richard made an awkward bow and glided off, much to the displeasure of his partner. A few days afterwards, he came running after her in the street and handed her a nosegay.

" I thought you might like these," he said,

"and besides, I want to tell you that I really wanted to dance with you, only it did n't seem quite fair. It was n't that I did n't want to," — which speech involved a supposition that put him more out of favor than ever.

A bluff old uncle of mine has told me of another trait of Beverly's.

" The fellow's mind," he said, " was —— unwholesome. Why, sir, if you undertook to tell him a decent story, he 'd stare as if you were talking to a woman."

My uncle's conception of decent stories, I may add, was of the robust old school.

Perhaps the most remarkable of Beverly's oddities, however, was of a very different kind. It was an amazing aptitude for the Italian language. To the inexpressible astonishment of the professor who introduced him to that musical tongue, he learned to read it in a few weeks, and to speak and write it in a few months, as well as the professor himself could. It seemed, Beverly said, like remembering something that he had known before.

"Per Bacco!" swore the professor, "his intellect is without limitation."

The professor, like some other men, had a convenient habit of measuring mental capacity by the ease with which people grasped his ideas.

There are a few more stories of Beverly's youth, which repeat the traits indicated in those which I have told. At the same time, when nothing happened to excite his morbid propensities, he seems to have behaved like a healthy boy. He was fond of exercise, and a good athlete according to the simple standards of the time. And he had as hearty a dislike of apron-strings as if there had been nothing odd in his character. He did not lack self-assertion either; it is remembered that when his querulous parent insisted that at twelve years old he must be followed about by a servant, he flatly refused to go out of doors unless he might go alone. All the same, I think Mrs. Beverly's excessive care repressed some of the robustness that was really in his nature.

2

When Richard was somewhat past twenty, Mrs. Beverly brought her earthly career to an end in the odor of sanctity. Then Richard, left without the care which had bored him while he still had it, fell into a gloomy state of mind. His mourning kept him much to himself; and his fortune was large enough to relieve him of the necessity of doing anything to increase it. American men of inherited wealth are now as plenty as grasshoppers; but in his day you could have counted them on your fingers; so it was held a fresh piece of eccentricity that he seemed determined, with rare fixedness of purpose, to do nothing in particular. Now nothing in particular is by no means good food for the mind; and he was soon so despondent that people began to shake their heads and talk about the paternal razor.

But I think that people were wrong. He always kept a singularly full journal; yet in the pages which were written about this time I find nothing to indicate any thought of suicide. His trouble seems to have been not a longing to escape from life, but a restless eagerness to do in life some duty which he could not see plainly.

"I cannot get rid of the idea," he writes, "that I am in the world for some definite reason. It is a common enough idea, they tell me. I was sent here to do my duty in general, they go on to say; it consists partly of church-going, and partly of making money as fast as possible, and partly of being either very radical or very conservative, as the case may be, on the question of slavery. Bah! Such commonplaces make me mad. It is none of them or of their kind that I look for. But I feel — I have grown to feel day after day and month after month — that I am here in this world of sunshine and darkness because I have a work to do, a work as real as a Messiah's. It is a work that no man but I can do; yet what it is I cannot tell. And the time may be passing; and the work may be left undone forever. Yet I can find no light, nor any seer."

Shortly after he wrote these lines in his journal he started on the travels from which he never returned.   Cleveland, the painter, who married our cousin, was already in Rome, one of the first of our countrymen to take up his professional abode there.   He wrote to Beverly sundry attractive things.   And one day Boston awoke to find that Richard Beverly had packed up and gone.

II.

HOW he crossed the Atlantic has little to do with us. Nor shall I pause any more than he paused in misty, green England, whose young queen had lately begun her reign; or in far-stretching France, where respectable citizen-monarchy still upheld the throne of pear-faced Louis-Philippe. His melancholy went with him. Other men looked with joy at the unwonted sights of the Old World; he seems to have found pleasure out of the question, for he was still tormented by his old perplexity. For what purpose was he come into this world through which he was journeying, he asked himself over and over again. England and France gave no answer; nor yet the grim Swiss mountains, with their rocks and their glaciers and their gaunt pines. But when at last he climbed the Alps and looked down upon

the land to which he travelled, a great flood
of happiness swept over him, — such happiness
as the old Hebrews felt when from the moun-
tain-top they gazed upon the fields that Heaven
had promised to their children.

" Italy's beauty," he writes, " begins with
Italy. Indeed, it should seem that some magic
dwelt in her name, and cast a veil of splendor
over all things that are permitted to bear it.
Why, it is worth while to come into the world
only to breathe such air as I have breathed
to-day. The lazy horses have droned along
the road. I would not have them speeded.
Had each step taken a century it would not
have been too long. The savage Alps are
behind me, though the country still heaves
with the same blows that drove the Swiss
rocks skyward. And perchance, if the magic
of Italy did not rest on this landscape, this,
too, would be as full of the grandeur of deso-
lation. But here no rock peeps out save from
a bed of verdure soft as a mother's breast. No

tree, no shrub, no green thing grows as if growth were labor. The curse of birth-agony seems stricken out of the world. Like the waters that leap down the mill-races, all Nature laughs here, even as she groaned in the Northern land. And she laughs a laugh of happiness, like the laugh of one who has eaten and drunk well, and who sits in the midst of his children, at peace with the world. Strange idiots with huge necks gibbered at us from their crazy barracks as we climbed the Alps. Here dark-eyed girls sit in their cottage doors, and glance roguishly at us as we pass; and when we look back they bend their heads once more over the spinning-wheel, with flushing cheeks. And we, finding no eye to meet ours, look further; and lose our thoughts among the vineyards, where vine and tree cling together as lovingly as virgin lovers meeting when the sun goes down. Nay, even misery itself laughs. Sturdy fellows, with vast brown breasts bared from boyhood to sun and wind, hang their heads and thrust out their hands for help. To-day I would give

alms even to a shivering Swiss. I fling coins
to these merry children of the land that shall
be mine henceforth. And I bid them laugh out
the laugh that I see hidden in their eyes; and
merrily drink to me, their brother who is come
home. For Italy is to all men a second fatherland, nearer than Heaven and not less lovely.
And it is a merry land. And life is a merry
thing."

Now all this is romantic, overwrought stuff,
if you please; but surely it is not morbidly
suicidal. And this is the sort of thing that
Richard Beverly wrote as he made his way
towards Rome. In this mood he came to merry
Milan, where even under the white-coated Aus-
trians all life seemed one long festival. There
he duly admired the dark, sleepy-eyed women,
with their fans and their mantillas; and the
great white cathedral. Then on to Bologna,
where he thought the Caracci great; but stood
beneath the Carisenda and watched the clouds
pass over the toppling pile, because Dante had

stood there and watched before him. Then
came ducal Florence, where he was full of
Dante again, as he saw the fair San Giovanni
that Dante called his own; and standing by
the stone where men say Dante sat of old,
looked up at the tower of Giotto. Here, too,
the paintings opened to him a new world of
beauty. Whence came the colors which the
dead masters laid upon their canvases, he wondered for a while in vain. Then, one evening,
as he stood at Fiesole and looked down the
soft valley of the Arno, the sunset light of
Italy came streaming up from the west and
told him.

Then he drove through the steep Etruscan
country and looked down on the Trasimene
lake; and saw Perugia perched upon her rocky
hill; and Assisi, with her vast piles of holy
masonry; and Terni, with her rushing waters.
And late one afternoon he came to Rome.

III.

IN those days the Cardinals were the greatest
people in Rome, except, of course, the Holy
Father, whose white mules still jingled past
churches and palaces and fountains. The Cardinals were something more than high priests.
One of them was sure to be, any one of them
might be, the ruler of the people who smiled or
frowned as they swept along, with stiff lackeys
and great umbrellas behind their lumbering car-
riages. And most of them were familiar figures.

There was one, however, who was little more
than a name to the Romans; and perhaps for
that very reason his name seemed fraught with
more dignity than those of the astute priests
whose faces and whose deeds were always meeting you. The Cardinal Giulio Colonna kept
within his own doors, save on those great occasions of state when all the pillars of the Church

were in duty bound publicly to uphold her splendor. With the active life of the time he had little to do; and when on rare occasions his venerable figure passed before the eyes of common men, it seemed more than any other to embody the apostolic dignity of the Roman Church. Other members of the sacred college sharpened their wits in far-reaching diplomatic contests; and spent what time they had to spare in endless intrigues, which all their cunning could not keep hidden, to bring themselves nearer the chair of Saint Peter. Giulio Colonna sat apart. Every day, men said, he passed hours in solitary prayer. His thoughts were more of the other world than of this; and devout people were not wanting who whispered that holy visions had opened to his living eyes glories that many of his brethren should never see through all the ages. When these devout people caught a glimpse of his face, they saw in the fixed calm of his features, and in the distant look of the eyes that had not grown so old as had his bent shoulders, something that betokened knowledge of things that other men only guessed at. As Dante's grim visage scared the children who thought they saw lurking in its wrinkles the grime of Hell, so the old Cardinal's deep eyes told believers that living men might still have glimpses of Heaven. So he lived and prayed apart from the world. And clever people said that he was very clever; and that his failing strength, together with his ever-growing holiness, was enough to insure him Pope Gregory's seat, if he only survived Pope Gregory. Some, indeed, ventured to hint as much, when his wily chaplain, Monsignor dei Bardi, was by. Whereat Monsignor, than whom no better man of business or of state wore violet stockings, would generally put his smiling head a little more to one side than usual, and would take a pinch of snuff, and utter through his thin lips some epigram clever enough to make those that hinted wish that they had held their peace.

Yet, if old stories could be believed, Giulio Colonna's life had not been one of unmixed holiness. Legends grow fast, to be sure, and perhaps the greater part of the story was a legend; but there was no doubt that in his youth the saintly Cardinal had been a man of war. No more gallant officer, in every sense of the word, had worn spurs and uniform in his early days. And when, soon after his brother's death had placed in his hands what was left of the Colonna fortune, he had taken to the Church, instead of taking to himself a duchess from among the Roman maidens who clustered about his ducal path, there had been a good deal of surprise, and no small amount of head-shaking. Something certainly must have happened to change a man of the world into a man of God. Perhaps it was a miracle. But the story that people whispered had nothing miraculous about it. Indeed, in papal Rome it was commonplace; but to us of the New World such tales are not commonplace as yet. And I am ardent enough to believe that more generations than are now behind us must have passed away before our land is old enough to hear without a start such tales as were whispered of Giulio Colonna.

When the century was still young, Pius the Seventh came back to Rome, and with him came those Romans whom the storms of the Revolution had scattered for a while. Things were to be, it seemed, as they had been before impious philosophy had turned away from salvation the thousands of souls who had risen against the Holy Church. But the old system needed more vigorous defence than it had needed in the quiet olden time. Roman nobles banded themselves together to protect the Mother Church who had watched over them and their fathers for a thousand years. And among these loyal gentlemen no one was more loyal or more active than the Duke Pietro Colonna, elder brother of Giulio, and head of the great house to which they belonged.

Pietro Colonna seems to have been an earnest man, not without mysticism in his devotion to the church from which the fortune of his race had sprung when some far-off great-uncle had been made pope, centuries ago. Like many earnest men, in passionate Italy as well as in our more phlegmatic Northern lands, he gave himself with all his heart to what he believed to be the truth. And having given his whole heart to the cause of the Church, he had nothing but punctilious politeness left for the beautiful duchess to whom he had given his name. Emilia Colonna, by birth remotely akin to him, was a wonder even in Rome, where women grand as goddesses have dwelt since the days when the Sabine beauties came to add their graces to the stout stock that had taken root by the Tiber. The splendor of her face and form has not yet died out of Roman drawing-rooms, where reflections of it still gleam faintly in the words of old men who knew those that knew her. But all this splendor was lost on solemn Duke Pietro, who thought of nothing but the grandeur of the Church, and the wicked plots of the Carbonari, — if, indeed, the Liberal plotters of those early days had already taken the name that they bore in times nearer our own.

A Roman woman claims more than formal homage from her lord. The beautiful Duchess Emilia could not rest content with the courtesy of her patriotic spouse. At least so thought the people of her time, who looked about accordingly to see whose love, of all those who pressed to offer her their love, should be rewarded with hers. What truth lay in their conclusions nobody rightly knew; but all Rome whispered, with no word of contradiction, that the beautiful duchess found close at hand the devotion that she vainly looked for in her marriage. The gallant Giulio, men said, played with her the part that Paolo played with Francesca in the Rimini that Dante knew. And so Rome lived and loved and plotted, as our century grew older.

The Liberal poison, whose workings gave the Duke Pietro so much concern, ran deep in Roman life. There were many gallant gentlemen to rally with him about the standard of the Church. But there were others who dreamed already of an Italy, dearer to them than any church, or than any of the states that then divided the country. There were men who told one another in whispers what Macchiavelli had written three hundred years before: " In great part, all the wars which foreign hordes have waged against Italy have been caused by these Roman priests; for the most part, all the barbarians who have surged in upon us have been called hither by them. And even in our own time they do their old work; and that it is which keeps Italy disunited and feeble."[1] There were gentlemen in Rome whose hearts were full of words like these. To speak them out, meant exile or life-long prison; so they kept them back, and whispered and plotted. Who they were, none but themselves knew, except perhaps, Duke Pietro's spies. But if rumor did not lie, Giulio could have told you.

---

[1] "Tutte le guerre che furono da' barbari fatte in Italia, furono in maggior parte dai Pontefici causate ; e tutti i barbari che quella inondarono, furono il più delle volte da quelli chiamati. Il qual modo di procedere dura ancora in questi nostri tempi ; il che ha tenuto e tiene l' Italia disunita ed inferma." — *Istorie Fiorentine*, Book I.

In Duke Pietro's own home, men said, were hatched the plots that he would give his life to suppress.

One night came a piece of news that thrilled through the city in an hour. Pietro Colonna had been stabbed to death as he was stepping from his carriage at his own door. The Duchess Emilia, who sat above, had uttered no cry. Cold as marble, she had sat in the flickering light looking down at his dead form. Then she had bidden them carry him into his palace; and, with a face as white as the dead man's, she had mounted to her own apartment. There she had turned about once, bidding the servants send Giulio to her, when he should come; and with no more words had passed within her doors. The news, as I have said, spread like fire through the city. It reached Giulio no one knew where. He came hurrying to the palace door; with a tremor in his voice, he asked if the tragic report were true. When they told him that it was, and that the widowed duchess waited for

him above, his eyes seemed to start from his
head, and he lifted up his arms and shook
his clinched fists in the air. Then he turned
and hurried away. He never spoke to Emilia
again. Within a month he had given himself
to the Church.

Meanwhile, the story goes, she sat waiting
for him who did not come. Finally, late in
the night she rang and asked if he had sent
her no word. When she heard that he was
come and gone, she bade her servants leave
her, with a firm voice. But before they had
passed her door they heard a fall; and turning about, they found her on the floor sense-
less. From that she went into a fever, and
for days they thought that she would follow
the Pietro whose name she kept calling in accents of warning and of terror. But she rallied,
and lived on in Rome, — more beautiful than
ever, save that her marble face grew to have
the hardness of marble. What her life was
the scandals of the time will tell those who
choose to know. At last her passions and her

sorrows came to an end. She died, and was
laid by the Duke Pietro's side in the marble
chapel where the Colonnas lie. And Monsignor Giulio, already famed for his holiness, came
and said a mass for her sinful soul.

And now the Duchess Emilia had been dead
for well on to five and twenty years. The
Colonna fortune had not prospered meantime.
The old Cardinal, in his great palace, thought
little of money matters; but those who lived
about him found that money matters necessarily
occupied a good deal of their attention. The
household was not large. There was Monsignor
dei Bardi, who devoted himself to His Eminence with a singleness of purpose accountable
for only on the supposition that he saw at the
end of his labors a vision of a red hat. There,
too, in apartments of their own, were the Countess Barbarini, a child of the Cardinal's dead
sister, and her daughter, the Contessina Filippa.
These the old man had taken to his home when
they were left with no fortune at the death
of the Count, whose life and money had been

dissipated in cards and other frivolities. In return the Countess, whose practical qualities rivalled those of the smiling chaplain, looked after what was left of the Colonna fortune with no mean skill. This Countess had been a beauty in her day ; and the Contessina Filippa, the only other member of the household, was said to be as beautiful a girl as ever grew into woman-hood in a Roman palace.

Of course, they did not need the whole palace for themselves. So, reserving two great suites and a picture-gallery, renowned both for its merits and for the fact that the foreign sight-seers who penetrated almost everywhere never penetrated there, the Countess and Monsignor between them had long ago managed to let the rest of the vast building to a motley array of lodgers, native and foreign, noble and ignoble. Among these lodgers was Cleveland, whose studio was not far off. And when Beverly came to Rome the artist insisted that he too should take quarters in the Colonna palace, where an apartment happened to be vacant.

IV.

FROM this time on, I shall tell most of Beverly's story in his own words as they were written in his journal. The passages I shall quote are not always consecutive; the second in this chapter, for example, comes some days after the first; the third some days after the second. But it was his habit to use so few dates that I have thought it useless to insert any. When I come to a passage which it seems best to omit, I shall indicate the omission by a space and some stars. How much time has elapsed between any two quotations I often know as little as the reader.

From Beverly's Journal.

If I am ever to be happy I ought to be happy here. I live in a Roman palace, of which, so far as my own rooms are concerned, — and my apartment is large enough for a prince, — I am master. There is nothing to prevent me from giving myself up to the delights of Rome; and these delights are no common ones. Here, all about me, are the ruins of the ancient world that I have dreamed about ever since I was a child. Here, too, are marble churches and palaces and fountains; here is the muddy Tiber with its bridges; here are villas and gardens, and columns from which the saints have toppled down the brazen emperors; here are statues and great paintings, and a thousand other nameless things which carry me at will through the whole length of the Middle Ages to our own days. With a few steps I can wander out of this troublesome modern time into a limitless past, of which nothing is left but the loveliness. It is the sin and the tumult and the passion of human life that die. Enshrined in art the beauty of the old days lives, and it will live forever. Here in Rome you have no excuse for thinking of mean and hateful things. Each palace door, each church porch, with its curtain ready to swing aside at a touch, leads you into some old world that has been purified of all that is not good.

If I want modern life, too, I have only to pass a staircase, and there I am at Cleveland's door. He and Cousin Abby do all they can to welcome me. He even leaves his painting and walks with me about this marvellous town, which has grown as familiar to him as old Boston is to me. He can lead me straight to the things that all men wish to see, just as I could lead him to Copp's Hill, where I used to ponder over the epitaphs and the carved arms of the old Tories who went away from New England when the King was driven out. And Cousin Abby has been very kind. She has saved me the trouble of engaging servants, by lending me some of hers; and she insists that I shall dine with her every night.

Yet here in Rome I find stealing over me that old feeling which I had hoped to leave behind me in the cloudy North. What right have I to be here, passing in listless pleasure the hours that have been given me to pass on earth? What meaning has my life? What right have I to live a life that has no meaning, a life that shall leave on the world no trace of its passing? Blessed are the obscure, they say. Blessed may they be, with all my heart. I have no wish to make a name, as they call it. But there is something — I have always known that there is something in this world that no one but I can do. And the time is passing. Thus to idle is to disobey the voice of duty, of conscience. Awake! Be doing! it cries to me day and night. I start up, longing for one word of counsel. Whither shall I turn? There is no answer.

Here in Rome I feel these things more deeply, I think, than I have ever felt them before. Perhaps a strange thing that is happening to me makes them seem more real. I am haunted. Day after day, hour after hour, there sweeps over me the sense that I am in a land that I have known before. Everywhere are vague memories, stretching towards me from a past —

a far-off past of mine — that has to do, I know
not how, with this Rome through which I walk.
These ruins, these churches, these fountains
have known me of old. They have known
more. They have known some secret that I
long to remember, a secret that fled away
from me in the past that had vanished before
memory began. I have forgotten; but Rome
remembers. And the sparkle of her sunshine,
and the rich mantling of her shadows, and the
misty spray of her fountains, and the rustling
of her trees, and the breath of her flowers,
and the placid faces of her marble men, all
strive to tell me what I should know without
the telling; but they tell it in a strange tongue,
and I cannot grasp their meaning.

I have talked of this to Cleveland and to
Cousin Abby. I am just come from them.

"I am sure, Richard," said Cousin Abby,
"that your digestion is out of order. I shall
send you up some rhubarb. I always keep rhubarb on hand. It is quite harmless, and — "

"Excuse me, my dear," interrupted Cleve-

land, "but I can't help observing that you are
talking nonsense. The thing is simple enough,
Beverly. It is nothing in the world but your
memory of school-books. I felt something very
like it when I came here first, only it took me
differently. It struck me as irresistibly absurd
that places where I could sit and smoke my
cigar unless a snuffy priest told me to throw it
away, should have the impudence to bear the
names that were beaten into me at the Latin
School. I am quite an authority on corporal
punishment still. I can trace the ideas that
olive-wood still suggests in my mind, to a ruler
that lay on the desk of a certain usher, whom
I have painted in various unpleasant characters
during the last few years."

"I cannot feel that you are right," I said,
"I have never learned any mysteries about
Rome."

"I never supposed that you had," said he.
"The human mind is so constructed that what
is once in it makes the deuce of a bother in
getting out again; and when it has disappeared

as a memory it turns up again as a mystery.
Besides, when you are out of sorts — "

" That is just what I said," put in Cousin
Abby, — " he needs rhubarb."

" All he needs," said Cleveland, " is to get
his nerves in order. He smokes too much."

I hardly smoke at all ; and told him so.

" You don't smoke enough, then," said he ;
" have a cigar."

I took one. It was very good. Perhaps he
is right.

.   .   .   .

How a human face sometimes flashes into a
corner of one's mind that seems to have been
kept empty on purpose for it. This afternoon
I walked out with Cleveland on the Pincian Hill.
He wished me to see the view of Saint Peter's.

" On a good afternoon," he said, " it is something fine. You look over the whole city, and
see the dome swimming in an ocean of blue
glory. Then you get behind some trees, which
make a tremendous shadow for a foreground.
It is theatrical, of course ; but sane people like

the theatrical. Besides, everybody goes to the Pincio of an afternoon."

So we went to the Pincian Hill. Cousin Abby would not go with us. She rarely goes out. She cannot see, she says, why she should if she does not feel like it; and she is sure that there is no pleasure for her in looking at any number of people whom she does not know and does not care to. So we left her with some worsted work that seems to satisfy most of the wants of her soul; and walked together in those marvellous gardens that look down on Rome.

All the world was there, Cleveland said. I suppose it was. At another time I might have had eyes and thoughts for it. Indeed, at first I thought I should have them to-day. But suddenly in the passing throng I saw a woman, — a young girl I suppose I ought to call her; after that I saw nothing else. She had a face and form that seemed to have gathered to themselves all the riches of life and beauty that have been gathering in Rome since the world began. As she walked, I felt more than I saw that hers was such a form as the women of old unveiled before Grecian sculptors. As the sunlight fell on her cheek, it kindled there such colors as the masters of painting have treasured up in the canvases that you see only here. It was as if one of those marble women of old had awakened into all the warmth and passion of living human beauty. For the flash of her great eyes and the deep breath that came through her red and parted lips told of the rich life-blood that throbbed in her veins.

I looked at her as I should have looked at a goddess. I knew nothing except that she was before me. Then she turned her eyes toward me, and I forgot to take mine away. Just then Cleveland looked up and bowed. Mechanically I did the same; and stood with bared head as she passed with her companion,—a stately lady, of whom I noticed nothing more. When they had passed, and I had regained myself a little, I asked Cleveland her name.

"Have n't you seen them before?" he answered. "Why, that is our landlady, the Countess Barbarini, and the Contessina Filippa. She is devilish handsome, is n't she? I should like to paint her."

And he — an artist, whose work we of New England think inspired — could find no better words than these, could feel no deeper thing than that this woman among women might serve him in his trade. I said no more. As soon as I could leave him, I came home. As I passed up the stone stairs, they seemed unlike the stairs that I have trodden here before; for they, no doubt, have been pressed by her feet and brushed by the hem of her garments. I dined alone. Since then I have been sitting in my own rooms, in dim candle-light, with no thought save for that wondrous form that has burned itself into my mind.

Filippa! Filippa! I have caught myself whispering, in no sentimental lover's tone, for she has not kindled in me the silly love that one reads about. But she has taken her place in

my life, along with the Goddesses of Greece and
the Virgins of this marvellous Italy. To see,
to have seen, such a form as hers makes it worth
while to have been born.

Filippa! — And Cleveland thinks her devilish
handsome and would like to paint her!

.   .   .   .

Cleveland is so good to me that I feel ashamed
of allowing myself to think and to write down
that he cannot see and feel as I do the wonders
of Rome and the beauties of life. It is not that
I am a finer being than he, I feel sure. It is
only that he is full of occupation, while I am an
idler. He has no time to play with his dreams.
I have no other thing to do. And so I soar up
into all sorts of clouds, and feel much offended
when Cleveland reminds me that he is walking
on solid earth.

To-day, when I went to his studio, I found
with him a sharp-faced American, deep in talk.
Cleveland introduced me to the man.

"Glad to meet you, sir," said he, shaking my
hand until I shook all over; "knew your father

well. You ain't engaged in manufacturing yourself, are you ? "

" No," said I.

" Perhaps you are in the art business, like
your friend here ? "

" I am not in any business," I said.

" Ain't ! " said he, with an air of disapproval,
and turned back to Cleveland, with whom he
was soon deep in some talk that sounded like a
bargain.

" Well, sir," he said at last, " you know what
such things are worth, and I don't. What I
want is something that people will allow to be
valuable, and I 'm willing to pay. No, I don't
want to see the concern. I can't tell one picture
from another ; but if folks that know what 's
what say that this one 's the thing, go ahead."
And with a nod to me he withdrew.

If I were an artist, such a fellow, I am sure,
would upset me for a day. I was silly enough
to feel annoyed that Cleveland took up his
brushes and calmly went to work as soon as the
door was closed.

4

"What do you suppose that æsthetic person is doing?" he asked, after a while.

"I have no idea," I answered.

"Something in agreeable contrast to himself," said Cleveland. "He is buying the Colonna Titian. It delights me, do you know, to think that a creature like that should have happened to be the means of getting me into a Roman gallery that hardly anybody in Rome has seen, — particularly when I have been living for a couple of years in the same house with it. The old Cardinal, you know, is very jealous of his pictures; and that Florentine priest of his is clever enough to know that things you can't see are more talked about than things you can. So until this patron of art came along with the idea of giving some Yankee museum a first-rate picture, I cooled my heels at His Eminence's door in vain. But as soon as they found that I really meant business they were all smiles. I am going to take you there in a day or two. I am saving it for a *bonne bouche.* After the Colonna gallery, where you have everything to yourself, all the others, where everybody runs against your elbows, are intolerable. There you have the real thing."

And as he painted, I sat and thought how strange a world this is, where the vulgar ostentation of an untaught fellow can serve to open for me the doors of that marvellous Roman girl, who passed before my eyes on the Pincian Hill.

V.

From Beverly's Journal.

I HAVE seen the Colonna gallery, the one great collection in Rome that is kept secure from the crowd. Surely no spot is better worth guarding. If there be sacred things in art, if there be a holiness about works into which men have poured all the beauty of their lives, that holiness is here. And just as I am offended to see careless travellers tramp through churches where they would disdain to kneel, so I shrink from passing with a careless company the works that the masters have left us. In the Colonna gallery each picture seems to have grown in its place as naturally as the churches of Rome, or the vines that wander over Roman ruins have grown up above the elder city. Each one is in itself a new glimpse into another world, — a world of happiness and of agony vast beyond words. I did not think of judging these marvellous things. I simply looked and marvelled. And in the end I was as one who has seen a vision ; who knows that he has been swept through endless space peopled with beings grander and sterner than men, and who wakes to find that memory cannot bear the burden, that it can keep for him only the fading knowledge that he has for a moment known things too holy to be profaned by common human thought.

Yet one picture I cannot forget, perhaps because it is to be carried away from this shrine where it has been treasured for three hundred years. It is the Titian which Cleveland is buying. It shows a woman seated on a great rock. At her feet grow flowers. Behind her is a glorious landscape where fantastic mountains rise up in a mist of blue as pure as a sunny ocean. Above her head is foliage which seems to rustle in a gentle wind. And the woman's grand form throbs and swells in every part with the full life-blood of old Italy. But she looks at none of the loveliness that is about her. With tear-

swollen eyes and trembling lips she gazes up
towards a Heaven that her sight cannot reach.
The agony of sin that may never be undone,
even though it be forgiven, is upon her. And
it should seem that the very richness of the life
which brought her to that sin makes the agony
greater, even as it strives to deaden it, to whisper back her thoughts to earth. For her fingers
grasp a skull. It is Magdalene.

I looked at this picture in silence. For the
moment I hardly saw its lines, or the marvellous
colors that Titian wooed from the skies of Ven-
ice. My heart was full of the meaning that was
beneath them, a meaning too deep for words. 1
thought of the vastness of sin in this world that
without it would be a paradise; of the vastness
of the mercy that brings men even through sin to
peace; of the vastness of the agony with which
that peace must be won. In this world few are
happy enough to pass through life unstained.
Men live thoughtlessly; and one day they awake
to find memory seared with thoughts that may
not be washed out. Then, in the moments of

solitude that come to us more and more as life goes on, we shrink from the self with whom more and more we must live, the self with whom at length we must pass out alone into the solitude of death. Blessed, verily, are the pure in heart.

Cleveland was beside me. He spoke at last.

" Wonderful, is n't it ? " he said.

" Wonderful ! " I answered.

" A few things like that will go a good way to civilize the Yankees," he went on. " Did you ever see such color? We can't do anything like it nowadays. I comfort myself with wondering how much of it is art and how much is chemistry. After all, nothing but time can give tone to painting. I have left some colors at the bottom of a picture or two for which I have great hopes in the twenty-second century."

I said nothing more. Cleveland's words had called me back to myself. They had called me back at the same time to the strange thoughts which had filled my mind when I first crossed this threshold. The feeling that I had known of old the things which I saw had swept over me more strongly than ever. Cleveland has told me often that he is the only stranger who is permitted to come here. In moments of sober thought I know that he speaks the truth ; but sober thought will not always come. As I looked at the great Titian, and as I gazed up at the ceiling where pagan gods sit on rolling clouds and smile at one another across the yawning cracks that have opened in the plaster, there came to me the overwhelming thought that I had seen all these things before, that I had known them well. How I had known them and when I could not tell. But with the feeling that I had known them there came a great sense of horror, of agony such as Magdalene felt as she sat and gazed heavenward. Such a feeling I never knew before. I trembled. I seized Cleveland's arm.

"Take me away," I said.

"There is a fine Domenichino that we have not seen yet," said he; "it won't do to waste a chance like this."

"Take me away," I said. "I have seen

enough." And I almost forced him to lead
me away.

As we passed out a great carriage drove into
the court-yard of the palace.

" By Jove ! " said Cleveland, " here is His
Eminence. We are in luck. You might have
stayed here ten years and never have seen him.
Stand aside and look at him. Ten to one, he
will be the next pope."

So we stood at the head of the great staircase and watched two figures slowly ascending
toward us. One was a tall priest with sharp
eyes, and clean-cut features set in a smile such
as hides the thought that may be behind it.
He walked with a firm step. On his arm
leaned the other, a bent old churchman who
moved with the infirmity of age. His head
was bowed down, as if the toil of climbing the
broad stairway was almost beyond his power.
Yet with all his weakness there was about him
such an air of dignity as I had never seen before. I watched him come up toward us with
a feeling like awe.

" He is a grand old fellow, is n't he ? " whispered Cleveland. " He is tougher than he
looks. He is younger, too. It 's not years
that have aged him, so much as fasting and
prayer and all that sort of thing. He has put
himself through enough of that, they say, to
kill an ordinary man twice over. But he
hopes to be pope, you know, and hope is the
elixir of life."

By this time they were close to us. Cleveland bowed low, and I followed his example.
The old Cardinal bent his head in return, and
lifted his hand with a gesture of blessing. As
he did so he turned his face toward us, and I
saw it for the first time. For the first time it
must have been, yet as I looked upon that face,
pale and thin, and trembling with age, and
marked in every line with a gentleness and
a holiness such as I had not dreamed that
human features could possess, it seemed to me
that in some far-off time I had known him, too,
even as I had known his grand dwelling. The
shudder, the horror that I had felt in the

presence of the Magdalene came upon me again. I gazed at the old man with what must have seemed brutal rudeness. I could not move my eyes from his face.

As I gazed at him, he turned his eyes toward me. Then he stopped for a moment and gazed at me with a look that was almost like a recognition. It seemed to me that he too felt something of the mystery that was upon me. His face grew strangely earnest. His eyes seemed to pierce me through and through. For a moment I thought that he was about to speak. But this was only for a moment. He raised his hand once more in blessing.

"*Pax vobiscum*," he muttered in a low voice. Then, leaning more heavily on the arm of his companion, he passed on, and we stood and watched his tottering steps and his bent shoulders.

. . . .

I cannot sleep. I have lain awake, it seemed for hours. Now I have risen. I have tried to read by the flickering candle-light that makes

these great rooms seem too mysterious to be
dwelt in by men. The words meant nothing.
I flung my book aside. My mind is full of
strange thoughts, — of the knowledge that I am
here on earth for some purpose which I cannot
see, the knowledge that has haunted me so long.
But now at last, as I strain my brain to catch
a glimpse of the things that are hidden from
me, I begin to see something more than the
smoky clouds that writhe about in that uncanny
world which men see when their eyes are closed.
I see the great Magdalene gleaming through the
cloudy mist in all the passionate glory that Titian
has wrapped about her. I see, too, the thin old
Cardinal, gazing at me with eyes that tell of
things that as yet I do not know. I stretch out
my arms. I hurry toward these forms. And
the smoky clouds writhe and curl, and I know
not whither I go nor what I am. But still I
am drawn on toward what I was born to do.
And before me I see waiting in the future,
beckoning me on, these shapes that in life I have
never seen before to-day. What is there that

binds them to me, that binds me to them? Whither do they lead me on? I cannot tell. But I cannot sleep. I cannot forget. I cannot think.

. . . .

To-day, when I was weary with the sleepless night through which I had watched, came word that the Cardinal Colonna would deign to see me. The message surprised me. They say that he keeps himself hidden from the world, that few may pass his threshold even of those whose names should give them a right to do so. Yet, after all, my surprise was not so great as I should have looked for. As I made my way toward him, it seemed as if I was going through places where I had been before; as if the stream of my life was carrying me with it whither it was used to flow.

I found him in a great room, hung with faded tapestry. He sat in a large chair, carved with strange figures. Satyrs grinned on the arms; and his long, thin fingers played about their shaggy heads, as he looked upon me with the

same deep eyes that had burned themselves into
my memory when I saw him first. When I
came to him he was not alone. The tall priest
was there, whom I had seen with him before.
His name, they tell me, is Monsignor dei
Bardi; he is a Florentine as wily as his old
countrymen of whom Macchiavelli writes. He
stepped toward me with the fixed smile that
never leaves his hard face, and led me forward
to present me to His Eminence. Another man
was taking his leave, a wiry, dapper little
creature, with a bald head and much vivacity
of manner. This, said Monsignor, was the
Prince Palchi, a rich gentleman of Rome. As
I came in he pressed his lips upon the sapphire
ring of the Cardinal, and passed out, ignoring
me as I might have ignored a child. Then,
when he was gone, His Eminence turned to
me.

"You are welcome to Rome," he said. He
spoke in French, and the words came hard;
his manner had the stiffness that comes when
men speak a language in which they cannot

think. But in spite of this his presence lost
no jot of its dignity. In our little New England we laugh at the greatness of the Old
World as a fiction of the past. We laugh at
it until we grow to think it a jest. When we
are brought face to face with it we are over-
whelmed with our presumption, like the scoffer
in the old story who found himself at last
embarking in the boat of Charon.

I stood in confusion for a moment. Then I
stepped forward to kiss his holy ring as I had
seen the Roman do. To such a man as this no
homage could be too reverent. But he drew
back his hand with a sort of shrinking.

"You need not pay me the honor that you
have seen the Prince Palchi pay me," he said.
"That is due to my office, not to me. And
you, they tell me, are of another faith."

I muttered some words that told him that I
am a Unitarian. I suppose I am; yet when
I compare the faint thing we call religion with
the grand church which declares itself true
everlastingly, everywhere, for all men, I am

not proud to own it. We are half-hearted Christians, we of New England.

"That shall not stand between us," he said. "I have sent for you because I wish to know you as you are."

I could say nothing. Why he should wish to know me I could not tell; yet it seemed right that he should. For in moments when I do not pause to think, I find myself fancying that there has been a dreamy old time when he has already known me, and when I have known him better than I know myself. I stood still.

Meanwhile, the Florentine priest stood by. I felt that he was looking at me, though I hardly turned my eyes toward him. I felt that he was studying me, and that behind that thin smile of his he was trying to make out what manner of creature his master had a fancy to know. He could not see the bond that drew us together. Of that I felt sure; for there are things that can never be seen by men who use the mind alone. Truly craftiness flings a veil across the eyes of the crafty; and men who would see what surrounds them in this great mystery of life must give themselves up to the seeing, nor ever ask themselves the wherefore of what they see. Yet though the priest stood without the secret he wished to penetrate, his presence troubled me. It troubled the old Cardinal, too. He turned to the priest and bade him leave us. Whereat Monsignor, never changing his smile, bowed and withdrew. But though he changed no muscle, it seemed to me that I could feel the spite with which he left us to an interview of which he could not guess the purpose. And as he passed out I heard the click of his snuff-box.

Then we were left alone, looking at one another; and the Cardinal Colonna was as full of nameless trouble as was I. For as he bade me sit in a stiff chair that stood near, his voice trembled with an emotion like that which quivered through me. Then he sat silent for a while; at last he spoke very slowly.

" They tell me that you have never been in Rome before," he said. " Is it true? "

5

I answered him in Italian, I cannot tell why. We had spoken before in French; but now the French words would not come to my lips.

" You speak our language," he exclaimed, with quick nervousness; " then you must have been here before."

I told him how lovingly I had learned his tongue in my own home; how it had come to me like something which I had known of old, just as Rome comes now.

" Strange," he muttered, half to himself. " In your infancy, in your childhood, perhaps, you were brought here. Memory has deep hiding-places."

I told him that until a few months ago I had never left New England; that my parents before me had never left it.

" Strange, very strange," he said again. And then he asked me many questions about myself, which showed me that in some way he had learned what little there is to know of my history. He had learned how I was born in that far-off Boston which seems to me now like a shadowy town in some unreal world; how I grew up there, an only child; how my parents were dead; how, at the bidding of my kinsfolk, I was come here for the first time; how I was filled with the charm of Italy; how Rome seemed to me haunted with memories. As he asked me if each of these things were true, I answered him that they were, with more and more marvel how he could know them.

"And these memories that haunt you here," he asked at last, "what are they like? Joyous or sorrowful?"

Then I told him, in such words as would come to me, how these strange feelings came surging upon me like dark mists, the shape of which I could not know; how they blinded my mind, and filled me more and more with trembling, I knew not at what; how each thing that seemed to me a thing that I had known of old made the mists roll more thickly, made the nameless terror greater; how through it

all I felt myself carried toward the work that
I have been made to do, — the work, the duty,
of which as yet I have no glimpse. Sometimes
it has seemed to me that my life-work was to
be a great one, admired of men; now, as it
draws nearer, it brings with it shapeless terrors
from which I fain would shrink. But ever my
life-current presses me onward amid these scenes
whose hidden meaning seems ever vaster.

As I spoke, the mystery of Rome gathered
about me more thickly than of old. I was
like one in a dream. I saw the old Cardinal as if he were afar off in his great chair;
and the shaggy satyrs of wood grinned like
devils, and tossed their horned heads, and
would have rushed upon me, but that he held
them back with his thin white fingers. Then
I saw his face, full of strange excitement, looking now at me, and now at something which
lay on a table by his side in a fretted frame of
gold. And none but the grinning satyrs knew
the meaning of what was passing.

Then I heard him ask me with slow words

where these strange fancies oppressed me most, what part of Rome seemed most charged with mystic meaning. And I told him how his great palace meant most to me of all I had seen; and I muttered words about the great Magdalene into whose heart my spirit had entered.

"And I," he said, in a voice so tremulous that the words would hardly come, — "am I, too, a thing that you have known?"

I could not tell. What I said I know not. All was confusion. It was as if I had slept.

When I awoke he was speaking words of comfort. The clouds of mystery were floating away from me. And he was grand and calm once more, as I had seen him first on the great stairway of his palace.

"Truly," he was saying, "your life is a mystery, a mystery full of sadness; but the time may come when the sadness shall be all past, when the mystery shall be all clear. Watch and wait. Come to me when you will. To speak out such things as are in your mind does men good. Do not fear to speak them to

me, for I have known joy and sorrow and agony,
and life has taught me to feel for others whose
burdens are heavier than mine — if so be it
such others there are — that sympathy which
should make their burdens lighter. Speak to
me when you will. I will always listen.
And perhaps this friendship which begins so
strangely shall end for you and me in a joy
that neither of us knows to-day. God grant
that such may be His will."

His words were like a message of peace. I
found myself kneeling at his feet, pressing my
lips upon the blue-veined hand that let me
grasp it now. Then I turned up my eyes
toward his. He was looking down at me, still
amazed. And it seemed to me that even as
we looked upon one another then we had looked
before; and though to look at one another now
brought peace to both, the thought of the looks
that we had cast upon one another in the nameless past brought back the shudder that had
swept over me when I stood before the Magdalene. My eyes looked into his; and he looked

down, first at me and then at something which he held in his hand. It seemed like a miniature. As he gazed at it the look of trouble came creeping over his face again; and he drew back his hand as if he shrank from my touch.

Then, with a great effort, he laid the miniature on the table beside him, with its face down so that none could see it; and his fingers grasped instead a golden cross that hung about his neck; and the look of calmness came back to his face.

" God be with you, my child," he said. " Come to me when you will. Such comfort as I can give, you shall have."

Then I left him alone in his carven chair. But the shaggy satyrs grinned no more, but gnashed their teeth in spite.

VI.

From Beverly's Journal.

FOR the first time since I was a child, my
life is neither a pleasure nor a burden ;
it is a fact, like the Tiber which I watched
to-day swirling under the Bridge of San An-
gelo ; like the Tiber, it is flowing onward
whither it knows not, but it is flowing as it
was made to flow. I am content.

I go to the Cardinal Colonna almost daily.
What draws me thither I know as little as
ever. I know only that in his presence I find
a semblance of the peace I yearn for. Yet
what I find there is not like the peace of the
blessed, that great contentment which comes
to happy souls when their work is done. It
is like the peace of one who has shuddered for
years in the fear that death may take him

unawares, and who finds himself at last face to
face with a fate that may not be shunned, and
breathes freely because the terrors of uncer-
tainty are past; yet all the time the death that
he sees before him is ever a vaster mystery.

Perhaps this feeling is foolish. I have tried
to speak of it to Cleveland; but he laughed at
me, and I said no more. Yet in his laughter
he explained one thing that had seemed wonderful. How the Cardinal Colonna had come to
know the history of my life I could not guess.
Cleveland laughed again when I said so. Monsignor dei Bardi, he told me, who is deep in
bargaining with him about the great Magdalene, had asked him many questions about
me. Doubtless, Monsignor had reported his
answers to the Cardinal before His Eminence
summoned me.

" Though why the devil His Eminence should
trouble himself about you," said Cleveland, " is
more than I can see. He never showed any
interest in us."

" And I'm sure," said Cousin Abby, " we

never wanted him to. The less you have to do with Romish priests the better."

Cousin Abby is a stanch Protestant; she goes to all the services at the British Legation, where decent English folk appear in black coats and monstrous bonnets.

They are kind to me, these kinsfolk of mine. I am grateful, I think, for their kindness; but in spite of myself they trouble me with their constant talk of little things. The meanness of life rises before me with every word they speak. And when I speak frankly to them they stare at me as if I were a madman. Perhaps while they stare they remember the old story of my parents. With them I find it best to keep my thoughts to myself. And thoughts kept back surge and swell in my mind longing to burst out, until I am in a great trouble; then, if I speak, my words are incoherent. So things go on, from bad to worse.

With the Romans whom I have come to know all is different. The movement of their life is like the current of a great stream whose source is hidden deep in a past forgotten by man, a stream which is flowing on toward some unseen future whither it is bearing all the world. And the life that I have known in New England, the life that my kinsfolk have brought with them to Rome, is like some tiny whirlpool, full of broken sticks and mean things, ever circling round and round in some petty corner of a shore that has caught it and keeps it apart from the stream.

Though I have seen the Cardinal Colonna so often I have never spoken of the mystery that was upon us when first we met face to face. Nor has he spoken of it to me. We talk of common things, — now of the old glory of Rome and the beauty that still thrives in Roman sunshine, now of the cold New England that has passed out of my life like a troubled dream, now of art and letters and men, — never of ourselves. Indeed, that solemn moment when he and I looked into one another's eyes and saw there we knew not what seems to me now like a dream, too. But it is like a dream from which

I am not quite awakened, a dream into which,
I know not how or when, I may fall again.

. . . .

I am beginning to feel that I have friends
here in Rome. The Cardinal Colonna has made
me known to the kinsfolk with whom he lives.
They have treated me with kindness. They bid
me come and go among them like one of themselves.

Thin Monsignor dei Bardi looked doubtfully
upon me at first. He would peer at me with
his small eyes, as he handled his snuff-box,
wondering whether I had some hidden object
in making my way among these people. But
now, I think, he sees in me no more than a
harmless caprice of His Eminence; and he glides
about as if I were not in the world. He has
smiles for all men, clever words for those who
wish them, supple bows for those who are
greater than he. Truly he is in the world if
ever man was. I smile now as I try to think
of him in the Heaven they preach about, where
business and smirking are unknown.

There is another man among these Romans
who treats me with small courtesy. It. is the
bald little Prince Palchi, who was with His
Eminence when I first came to him. The
Prince, they tell me, is the richest of modern
Romans. His father, who sprang no one knows
whence, made a great fortune in the troubled
times that came to all Europe after the Revolution in France. When he died he was a great
banker ; and left his bank and his money and
his palaces and gardens to his dapper son. So,
favored by fortune, the small prince lives among
men whose names run back to the days of the
Cæsars; there he makes formal bows, and shows
his white teeth in forced smiles, and plays with
his jewelled rings and charms, and prattles the
gossip of the hour, and has little thought for
men like me without a pedigree. But to the
great people of Rome he is cap in hand, and
when they deign to listen to what he says,
he looks vastly contented.

The one whom I see listen most is the Countess Barbarini. She stands at the head of the

house before the world, for the Cardinal Colonna
never leaves his own rooms, where none may
come unless he bids them. She is such a figure
as my fancy makes those women who ruled the
Popes in the olden time. Olimpia Pamfili-Doria
might have been like her, with her yellow laces,
and her big eyes, and her disdainful lip, and her
plump hand with tapering fingers. She is kind
to the people about her, but she treats them all
as if they were made of meaner clay. Indeed,
I might have thought her disdainful of all things
except herself, had I not seen her once in the
ante-chamber of the Cardinal Colonna, glancing
at some accounts which a white-haired servant
had laid before her. As I passed through the
room, I heard her exclaim, —

"What is this? Fish!"

"For the table of His Eminence," said the cring-
ing servant. "The Holy Apostles themselves
could not have bought it for a lower price."

"Nino!" cried the Countess, "if ever you
expend such a princely fortune on fish again,
not all the Holy Apostles themselves, if they

came hat in hand, should prevent me from turning you from my doors."

So, after all, there are things in life which the stately Countess deigns to notice.

Among the men I see in her presence there is one to whom I feel already as if he were an old friend. This is the Count Luigi Orsini, a godson of the Cardinal Colonna's. He is a favorite with His Eminence, and comes and goes here as if this were his home. His race is among the oldest of Rome. He is an officer in the Pope's guard. Sometimes he comes in a uniform as grand as ever a school-boy painted with his first box of colors. He is full of youthful life ; but the training of the world he lives in keeps him calm in manner. And perhaps I might have thought him as cool as Monsignor himself, were it not for the warm grasp of his hand, and for the fire with which he spoke to me one day some verses of a Roman poet whose name I had never heard. Monsignor dei Bardi chanced to be by. As he listened to the verses his smile was not pleasant.

"Your poetry is very charming, Count," he said at last, at the end of a stanza; "but if I were you I think I should prefer my uniform. The two do not seem to me compatible."

"I am an Italian!" exclaimed the Count Luigi, with all the warmth which the verses had kindled. "No Italian can hear those words without a thrill."

"They do not excite my enthusiasm," said Monsignor drily. And when I had declined his proffered snuff-box, and he had taken a pinch in his discolored fingers, he moved away, gently shaking the brown dust from his hand.

"That black fellow is a serpent," whispered the Count, as Monsignor passed out of hearing ; "he has no blood in his veins." The Count's blood was burning red in his dark cheeks.

And Filippa—I wonder why I have left her till the last. I used to think that women had no charm for me. At home, I am sure, they had none. There they are good and pure, — better, perhaps, by the stern standards our ancestors fixed than she whom I love to think of here. Yet sometimes I like to fancy her among them, with the grand fulness of her human life gleaming beside their fading Northern beauty. By her side they would seem like feeble copies of what they were meant to be, as a Roman statue looks when it is stood beside a Grecian goddess. Her manner is simple, simpler than the manner of lesser women. Yet as she was when I saw her first on the Pincian Hill, when floods of sunshine filled the air, and the great dome of Saint Peter's was bathed in a mist of golden blue, and faint music came with the wind that rustled through the trees and the flowers, so she is here in the dark palace of her fathers.

In wild moments I have dared to think of her as mine, to dream of clasping her in my arms, or rather of sinking down before her and flinging my arms about her knees while she looks down, grand as ever, but with no forbidding gaze. But when I try to think of her with me, in the simple life that men and women live together in my country, I laugh

aloud. The Grecian goddess was no house-wife.
Yet is she the less to be adored for that?

Do I love her, I wonder? As I write the
words I laugh again at myself, but it is with
no happy laugh; for with the laughter comes
the old thought that will not be laid to rest.
Even here, where all things seem full of peace,
I feel that I am ever moving on, as the rolling
earth moves on through the space where there
is nothing to check its moving, toward my
duty that lies hidden. When that thought
comes I know that to my life, whirling onward
toward I know not what, I may never link
another, even though that other were a thousand-fold less precious than hers of whom I
love to dream. Yes, I should count it a blessing that she has never smiled on me, save
with the courtesy which she shows to all who
are about her. For whither I go I must go
alone.

.   .   .   .

To-night the past seems far away, the future
near; the past seems dark, the future bright.

I am like one who is awaking from a sleep that has brought no rest. In God's name, let me doze no more!

I am just come from the rooms of the Countess Barbarini, whither I was bidden along with the Romans who have come there of right all their lives long. There I was silent, for I felt little inclination to mingle with the company about me. I stood aside, watching the courteous men and the stately women, calm until they spoke, then speaking with volcanic fire. Among them I saw Filippa. From her my eyes cannot long depart when she is within my sight. So I stood and watched her face as she sat near by, not knowing that she was watched. By her side was small Palchi, whose bald head, with its fringe of crisp and perfumed curls, gleamed in the light of the tapers like the jewelled rings which I could see as he moved his hand. He was talking to her with animation, smiling and bowing and gesticulating as vigorously as the innkeepers with whom my vetturino squabbled on the road to Rome. But she listened with an air in which I saw at last some shade of her mother's disdainful look, and played with her fan, and looked about as carelessly as if she sat alone.

By and by her eyes met mine ; and it seemed to me that I saw in them a look of pleasure, as if she were glad to know that I was by. But her eyes did not rest on me, but wandered on toward others. And I stood, wondering for the first time whether the thoughts of her which more and more fill my mind had shown themselves unknown to me. Women, they say, look deep. If she has seen my heart, she has seen things that as yet I have not dared tell in words even to myself.

Presently she looked toward me again. Then, more than before, I saw that her look was friendly. So I passed to her side and spoke I know not what formal words.

When I came she held me out her hand, and I, for the first time, bowed over it and kissed it, as I had seen the Romans do. Then, as I rose up again and looked into her face, I saw

that she was looking at me with no displeasure ;
but she looked at me no longer than a maiden
should. I felt a throbbing in all my veins.
Standing by her side I knew only that I was
there. I spoke stiffly, for no thought would
come to my mind save that I must not speak
what I felt. And Palchi, who never left his
seat, tried to turn her from me, with fine compli-
ments; but she turned away from him instead,
hardly deigning to answer the talk which he
rolled off as glibly as if it were a lesson that
he had just learned. Yet she listened with a
smile to the nothings that I stammered, and
answered them as simply as they were spoken.
And it seemed to me that just as I was happy
with a troubled joy at her side, so she was
happy at mine ; that if Palchi had risen and
gone she would have been as glad as I.

But Palchi would not go. And presently
came her stately mother, who spoke to me so
that I could stay by Filippa no longer. I
turned to speak my farewell. As she answered
me she let fall some flowers which had been in

her hand ; and kneeling to pick them up, I took one and kept it hidden. Whether she knew what I had done, I cannot tell; but in her look as she bade me farewell there was no displeasure.

So, after I had spoken with the Countess Barbarini and with others who were about her, I came away. And here I sit writing of Filippa, thinking of her, forgetting the self that has haunted me so long. The thought of self comes, as old habits will, in spite of all we can do; but when it comes to-night I look at the flower which she has held in her hand. I kiss it, speaking her name. Then I think of nothing but of her.

. . . .

So my life glides on in Rome, now with my own kinsfolk, now with the old Cardinal Colonna and his. All things seem to smile, even the Roman girl who more and more fills my thoughts. In truth, Filippa is so full of gentle courtesy that I begin to dream of a time not far off when I shall dare, after the manner of her country, to speak of what I feel to those who may grant me the right to speak of it to her. Yet even in her presence, where I am filled with such love as makes me forget all other things, there comes to me little peace. The old feeling that I strive to trample down rises above all, and bids me gaze onwards toward the duty that I cannot discern nor yet forget. There is within me a voice which whispers that this passion to which I yield myself up is a devil's snare. In wiser moments I reason with myself, thinking how men who love are always tortured with disquiet until their love is blest; and I laugh at my folly as others would laugh. But my laugh sounds hollow.

When I come to the old Cardinal Colonna all is changed. In his presence I find a peace that I never find elsewhere. Yet even that is only such peace as a soldier finds when he lays him down with his arms upon him, never knowing when the order may come nor whither it may bid him go. From the Cardinal I am just come; and I feel still some remnant of the peace which his presence sheds about him. But now again the form of Filippa rises before my eyes; and there is a part of me that will think of nothing else, just as there is another part which bids me turn my eyes another way.

As I write these lines the clouds that I dread are gathering before my eyes once more, — the clouds wherein sits Magdalene, groaning in all the misery of her guilt. I seem to know that it is to her side that I should press on, nor rest beside this siren girl of old Rome. But now, again, I look upon the flower that I found at her feet, and I kiss it, murmuring her name; and in that murmur all other thoughts are drowned.

VII.

From Beverly's Journal.

I AM in a great trouble. I have let myself wander from the path that I should tread. I have striven to silence the voice that called me back. Even now I would fain be weak: I would fain tell myself that I have been betrayed, that the girl upon whom I have let my thoughts dwell has played with the honest love which she saw hidden in my eyes, that it was to spite dapper Palchi that she smiled upon me first, that then it pleased her fancy to see so strange a creature as I lying at her feet. But now at last I am gaining strength enough to blame my folly and no deed of hers, for the trouble I suffer.

To-day I was making my way to the Cardinal Colonna, thinking as I went of the peace that I

have found in his presence. I came to the ante-
chamber through which those who go to him
must pass. There I found an open door; and
looking through it, I saw sitting in an inner
room the Countess Barbarini. She was busy,
as I had seen her before, with household matters,
of which she talked to her old servant. Near
by sat Filippa, whose presence brought back to
me thoughts of love. So I stopped for a while
where I could not be seen, and looked at her,
marvelling, as I have always marvelled when
she passed before my eyes,.at the beauty which
is hers.

For a while I fancied that she sat alone, thinking I knew not what girlish thoughts. And it
seemed to me that I had never seen her face so
full of life and of passion, that I had never seen
such meaning in her eyes. I wondered at what
her fancy looked. In my foolish heart, I dared
to guess that it was I; and I longed to pass
within the room and to stand where she could
see me. But presently I saw her lips move as
if she spoke in a whisper to one who was near

but hidden from me. I felt my heart beat fast
as there came to me the thought that there
might be another to whom she looked and spoke
thus, as never save in my fancy had she looked
or spoken to me. I moved myself a little, to
see if perchance there was any one by her side.
And when I came where I could see who was
there, it was with a great effort that I kept myself from crying out in rage.

For beside her sat one who is suffered to
come and go here as if he were her brother,
though no tie of kindred binds them. It was .
the Count Luigi. While the Countess Barbarini's back was turned, and she was busy with
matters that filled her mind, he was whispering
to Filippa. None but she could hear his words ;
but though I could not hear them I could guess
their meaning. For no man speaks with such a
face, and no woman hears with such blushes, any
words but words of love. Then, if I could have
wished for more to tell me that what I guessed
was true, I saw him take her hand in his. And
she, glancing at her mother to make sure that

her eyes were elsewhere, suffered him to take it
and to press it to his lips.

When I saw that, I could look no more.
I stood aside where none could see me from
within. I leaned against the wall, full of passion such as those feel who have murder in their
hearts. Within myself I cried out that she had
tricked me, that she had played with the love
that had taken possession of my being. Then,
with no pause for thought, I took from my
bosom a little packet in which I had wrapped
the flower which when she first smiled on me I
had taken at her feet. I looked at it once, full
of rage. Then I flung it down and trampled
on it, doing dishonor to her who smiled as she
played me false.

But then came other thoughts. Was not this
sight that I thought I had seen only another
strange fancy, like the cloudy dreams of fate
that I had striven to forget? Was it in truth
the girl that I had dared to love and the man
that I had grown to deem my friend, whom I
had seen within, clasping one another's hands?

I rubbed my eyes; and gathering up my courage, stepped again to a spot whence I could see them.

All was as it had been before. The stately Countess still sat talking of money to her servant. Behind her still sat the lovers, with no eyes now save for one another, their hands still clasped together, their lips still moving with whispers that I could not hear, their cheeks still flushing with the happiness that I might never know.

Then, shrinking back, I trampled once again on the withered flower that I had loved to kiss. And so I turned away from them, who cast no look on me; and with unsteady step I made my way to the room where the Cardinal Colonna is used to sit. He had bidden me come when I would, and not trouble myself with any announcement of my coming. So, as had grown my custom, I passed within the door-way, and looked for the gentle figure that should sit ready to breathe upon me such comfort as I yearned for. But his great carven chair

was empty, and the footstool that stood beside
it was overturned as if he had arisen in haste.
And it seemed to me, when I found that he was
not where I had looked to find him, as if all the
world were bound to spite me. Like a peevish
child I was about to cry out. But of a sudden
I saw where he was gone ; and I was awed into
silence.

For across the great room there stood a carven
cross, on which was the form of Christ in the
great agony that he suffered for the sins of men.
And before it, on a wooden form such as I have
seen in the common churches, knelt the old Cardinal. His eyes were fixed upon the image ; his
face was turned away from me. But I could
see his thin white hands clasped tight together,
and I could hear the low voice in which he
breathed forth a passionate prayer.

I stood and watched him with such feelings
as have come to me when I have entered a
great church, where in the dim light I have
found myself of a sudden standing before the
priests of God, breathing the incense and list-

ening to the mystic words of the mass. The pettiness of the things that had worried my heart made me ashamed. The thought of the woman whose earthly beauty had dazzled my eyes until they could see no other thing, seemed as nothing in the presence of this man, who, more than any other that I have known, deserves the name of holy. For as the years have borne him on nearer and nearer to the end of the pilgrimage of his life, he has kept himself more and more apart from the things that men love. His mind is fixed on Heaven. In the midst of this Old World which my countrymen would teach me to think full of evil, he has moved. ever onwards toward that oldest world which Rome, with all her weakness and her wavering, has ever kept in sight, even as Peter kept his Lord. And now I found him here, face to face with the Master to whom he has given his loyal life.

For a while it was enough to stand and watch him. At last there came to me a great desire to kneel at his side, and there pour forth a confession of the weakness that had let me turn

from the path I was made to tread. I longed to
speak a prayer that I might forget the love that
for a moment had filled my heart, — a prayer of
blessing upon that other love which shall make
Filippa's life happy, whatever fate may come to
me. I longed to pray that, like the man who
knelt before me, I might have strength to press
onward to my work which some day I shall
clearly see; to pray, too, that the day when
my life-work shall no longer be a mystery
be not long in coming. So I stirred myself;
and with soft step, lest the sound of my presence should disturb him, I moved toward his
side.

The great chair where he was used to sit was
in my way; and at its feet there lay on the
marble floor something that sparkled. When
I came close to it I saw that it was the little
frame of gold that he had held on the day when
I first came here to his presence. It lay there
as if it had fallen when he had risen up. What
image that frame held I had never seen. I had
done better to pass it by without a look; for as

my eye first caught sight of it, I felt creeping
through me such horror as came to me when
I looked upon the Magdalene who could not
cast away her sin, — such horror as I felt
when first I knelt at the old Cardinal's feet.
Yet, though I seemed to know that what I
wished to see was an evil thing, it charmed me,
as sin charmed our fathers in the garden of
Paradise. I stretched forth my hand and took
the frame, and looked upon what was within
it. Then I stood still and trembled.

For there in the golden frame was the painted
figure of a woman, dressed in the garb that women
wore when the old Cardinal was young. Her
dark eyes looked upon me with a look that I had
known before. At first I could not tell where
I had known it. But then, of a sudden, I knew
that her face was mine, — that mine was hers, —
that the eyes that looked upon me from the
painted face were the eyes that had looked upon
me from my mirror ever since memory began.

Then more than ever I knew — I could not
tell how — the vileness of my life, breathing out

its time with no good deeds, droning useless
through the earth where it was made to work.
The great eyes of the portrait bade me be
doing. But what? — what? I could not tell.
I cannot tell. Within myself I cried out, " Be
merciful, Lord, to me a sinner!" But I made
no sound. And as I stood trembling, there
came to my ears the words of the old Cardinal's
prayer: —

" Save me, O Lord. Take my thoughts from
the things of this world to Thy holy will. Give
me strength to cast off the evil memories of the
past that I have striven to trample down within
me; to look to Thee, to Thee alone, in the infi-
nite goodness and mercy that Thou hast promised them who give themselves to Thee."

Then I knew that this was no place for me to
stay. And very quietly I turned away and left
the old man in the midst of his prayer. But all
the time I held the portrait in my hand. I have
it with me now. As I look upon it and see
again my own face, I am filled ever with a
deeper horror. What meaning lies within it I

cannot tell. But it has a meaning which shall not long lie hidden. The painted eyes look upon me with a warning that the work for which I was born is at hand. In God's name, let it come quickly!

VIII.

FOR some time after this entry there are few coherent words in Beverly's faded old journal. Indeed, I thought for a while that there was nothing to show what happened to him in that Roman world — so near us in time, so far away in all things else — until he began to write again with such calmness as it was his lot to know. One day, however, I found among some papers of my father's a packet of letters from Cleveland. One or two of them throw light on Beverly's story ; and it seems to me that I cannot do better than give here the passages that have told me all I know of what happened now.

"A queer thing has happened to Beverly," writes Cleveland, "after the fashion that queer things have of happening to queer people. I

sometimes think that our ideas of the commonplace are only the quintessence of our own pe-
culiar sort of queerness. A Roman studio is my
bread-mill, for example; and you probably find
it hard to imagine a life that is not busied with
making cotton and money up on the Merrimac.
But I must come back to Beverly, or they will
be making you pay double postage.

" I told you how he had been taken up by the
Cardinal Colonna, who has never been known to
do anything civil to a foreigner before. We
have lived here in his palace for a couple of
years, and it is as much as ever that we have
seen him drive out in his coach. In fact, all the
Romans are ridiculously exclusive. I do not
imagine that they exclude us from a particularly
amusing society.

" Why the Cardinal should have taken a fancy
to Beverly I could not quite see. But as I had
happened to be in a way of letting his chaplain
know that Beverly had a comfortable fortune,
I thought it possible that they had a notion of
making a match for him with a handsome young

woman, who is a niece of the Cardinal's, and has
no dowry to speak of. This seemed improbable,
though ; Romans have great ideas of family, and
do not appreciate that we have such a thing as
social distinction without titles. Seriously, I
don't believe that they understand the differ-
ence between me and a common native copyist.

" Beverly's queer adventure explains the
whole matter. A few days ago he came to me
with a disturbed countenance, and demanded a
private interview. So we sat in conclave in my
studio ; and there, with much mystery, he pro-
duced a miniature which, as nearly as I can
make out his rather incoherent story, he seems
to have stolen from the Cardinal Colonna. Of
course I shall make him return it.

" The miniature was the portrait of a woman,
painted thirty or forty years ago. When Beverly showed it to me I saw nothing remarkable
about it except a curiously familiar look. I
could hardly have seen the original, yet the face
struck me as one that I knew perfectly well. I
asked him who it was. He said that he did not

know. Whereupon I remarked that it was very well painted.

"' Whom is it like ?' he said, interrupting me.

"' I don't know,' said I.

"' Look! look!' he exclaimed rather wildly. So I looked; and all of a sudden I saw that the face was curiously like his own.

" The likeness was not in feature nor in color; it was in expression, — in what I call *type.* You know I have always had a theory that if you got together a dozen people of any race you please, from Italians to Esquimaux, taking care that no two of them looked alike, and then carefully studied each face, you would have classified humanity. Everybody you meet will look like one of the lot. In other words, the chance that one man will look like another is about one in twelve. Of course in this hybrid nineteenth century most people will look like two or three others. Nothing is rarer than a pure type. Now, the one thing that has chiefly impressed me in Beverly is that his face is as purely typical in its own way as Napoleon's was in another. And this woman, whose picture he had found, was a remarkably pure example of the same type as Beverly's. As far as I could judge from the portrait, they were no more alike in feature than you with your Roman nose and I with my pug. All the same the likeness was really startling. It is not surprising that Beverly, who has not paid much attention to this sort of thing, thought the resemblance uncanny.

"Indeed, I could not make him understand my view of the matter, though in order to explain it I sketched two or three types in a way that seemed to me rather good. He insisted that there was some hidden mystery about the likeness, and that the Cardinal Colonna knew what the mystery was and would not tell. The Cardinal, it seems, has had a way of looking at this picture when Beverly was about, and has acted as if he attached a good deal of value to it.

"Here, I thought, was a clue. I examined the miniature with care. The frame was sur-

mounted with a ducal coronet. The Colonna
arms were worked into it. In a moment it
flashed across me that this was the portrait of the
beautiful Duchess Emilia, the wife of the Cardinal's brother. They say that the Cardinal was
once her lover. The story is rather interesting."

And here Cleveland goes on to tell the story
of the Duchess Emilia, much as I have told it
already.

" The whole matter is clear enough now," he
concludes. " The old Cardinal, whose wits are
pretty well worn out with praying and waiting
for the chair of Saint Peter, has been carried
away with the likeness between the dead Duchess
and Beverly. Probably he has a misty sort of
idea that Beverly is her son and possibly his.
I explained this to Beverly. He said nothing;
but shook his head incredulously, and seemed
dreadfully shocked at the naughtiness of his
double. He is not in a healthy state of mind."

The rest of this letter has nothing to do
with Beverly. Another letter, however, gives

a glimpse of him and of what was going on about him. I do not know exactly when it was written. It is dated simply "Wednesday," after a fashion affected by Cleveland, who avoided formulas which suggested the commercial traditions of his family. On the whole, I think that it was probably written some little time after the next entries which I am going to quote from Beverly's journal; but in a narrative so fragmentary as this chronological order is of little importance. I think that Cleveland's second letter may best be put here.

"I am sorry to say," he writes, "that we have had a misunderstanding with Beverly. I hardly know who is to blame. Abby began it, I suppose; but really he had no business to take offence. For the rest, it does not amount to much. By the time this reaches you there will doubtless have been a grand reconciliation.

"Abby, you know, is a tremendous Protestant, — a good deal more of one than she used to be at home. For here she sees hardly anybody except travelling English people, who are inclined to believe that the Pope is Anti-Christ, and that all priests have cloven hoofs. They are fond of being presented at the Vatican all the same, — perhaps from a natural desire to get a notion of the lurid surroundings from which their apostolic faith is sure to deliver them in the next world. So Abby hates a priest, with a beautifully simple hatred.

" When Beverly took to going to the Cardinal Colonna's she was much alarmed for his spiritual welfare. She had no doubt that they were trying to pervert him, as she expressed it. I did not think her idea very plausible, and told her so. Beverly is not worth the trouble of a full-blown cardinal. His fortune might deserve the attention of a third-rate monsignor, but certainly not of a more exalted personage. But Abby is remarkably feminine. She does not often have an idea of her own ; and when she gets hold of one, I think it improbable that the devil himself could shake it. Reasoning is to her what a shower is to a duck. She is inclined to believe that the Cardinal Colonna had the mysterious picture painted for the special purpose of luring Beverly into the Romish fold.

"A few days ago they had it out in spite of me. Beverly came to dine with us. He had been at the Cardinal Colonna's during the day, and happened to mention it. Whereupon Abby began to dilate upon the errors of Romanism and the trickery of priests. Finally, she declared her opinion that he was in great danger. He flushed, and professed not to understand her. She proceeded to state that in her opinion the Cardinal Colonna was laying snares for his soul.

"'You are quite wrong,' said Beverly. 'The Cardinal Colonna has never spoken to me of religion.'

"'He will not speak to you,' said Abby. 'He is too crafty. He will act upon you without your knowing it.'

"'If so,' said Beverly shortly, 'so be it.'

"'Richard,' said Abby, with much solemnity, 'your danger is even greater than I thought. I must protest against your entering the Cardi-

nal's doors again. Heaven knows what may
come of it.'

" ' Then,' said Beverly, ' we will leave it to
Heaven. I must beg you to say no more.'

" But Abby would not be silenced. She went
on to produce some tracts with which she had
been furnished by an Anglican parson. And
before I knew it, Beverly had arisen and stalked
out of the room in a dudgeon, followed by
Abby's not very conciliatory assurance that she
should pray for him.

" This was bad enough. He has not been
near us since. Still, I was not mixed up in it.
The next day, however, as luck would have it,
came another difficulty, which embroiled me.
You know that I have been negotiating with
the Colonnas for a Titian. A man named
Slocum, from Providence, wants to buy it.
You know him, I think, in a business way.
Well, after no end of trouble I had arranged
a bargain which seemed satisfactory ; but when
it came to making the final arrangements there
turned out to be a difficulty. Slocum wanted

to pay in the damaged kind of currency that most Italians are contented to put up with. The Countess Barbarini, a vicious old harridan if ever there was one, insisted that the price should be paid in gold. Things came to a standstill again ; and bargaining enough began to delight the souls of all the dead Yankees. Beverly happened to hear of the affair. He was in my studio one afternoon when Slocum called. As soon as Slocum was gone Beverly declared that he would buy the picture himself rather than have it desecrated by such chaffering. It is a fine Magdalene, a remarkable piece of coloring which has taken Beverly's eye. He requested me to tell the Countess that he would pay her price. Of course I was in duty bound to warn Slocum. And Slocum thereupon offered to pay a lot more. ' He did n't propose,' he remarked, ' to let nobody get ahead of him.' Evidently he would pay as much as anybody else would offer. There was no sense in using Beverly as a cat's-paw. So I arranged matters for Slocum and wrote to Beverly that he had been outbid.

"He sent me back a single line: 'It is best as it is, I suppose.' That was all. He has not come near me since. You would fancy that I had done him an injury.

"Slocum's behavior about the Titian is diverting. He has paid a round sum for it without a murmur. Now he is making arrangements to send it home by a third-rate sailing ship from Civita Vecchia, because that will save freight. It would cost him fifty or seventy-five dollars more to send it safe by a regular line.

"By the way, it is certain that the Colonnas had no idea of capturing Beverly for their handsome niece. She has just been formally betrothed to the Prince Palchi, a sort of Roman Rothschild. He has a fortune big enough for three; his grandfather was a peasant. He wants blood; the Colonnas want money. It is a capital match."

And then Cleveland wanders off to other matters. Of Beverly he says no more. Nor does Beverly's journal speak of him for some time to come. The breach which was opened by the well-meant meddling of Mrs. Cleveland and the perfectly business-like behavior of her husband seems never quite to have closed. I suspect that the Clevelands were more to blame than the artist's letter would indicate. To have their kinsman walk over their heads into a society from which they were excluded was certainly annoying. Probably they showed their annoyance without meaning to. But it is not worth while for me to waste time in speculations.

One word, however, I may add to this chapter. Mr. Slocum's Magdalene never reached America. The ship in which he sent it from Civita Vecchia sprung a leak in mid-ocean. There she was met by a steamer, which saved her crew and left her to her fate. So the great Titian lies at the bottom of the Atlantic.

Now I must come back to Beverly, whose journal begins to grow coherent once more.

IX.

From Beverly's Journal.

EMILIA COLONNA! — until Cleveland spoke the name I had never heard it. Yet it echoed through my mind, raising up answering thoughts, as a trumpet-blast, they say, rouses the fading memories of an age-worn soldier. These thoughts are all confused; but I can see enough to know that they are no thoughts of peace. And strive how I may I cannot lay them to the rest whence they have sprung into being. It is a mere guess of Cleveland's which tells me that the face of this portrait that lies before me, the face that I have known as mine, is the face of the sinful woman who lived and died here before I came into the world, — for she died, they tell me, in the very year in which I was born. It cannot be, men would say, that in the life through which I have

8

moved hither from the quiet places where first
I looked on the light, her being can have had to
do with mine. Yet day by day and hour by
hour I am growing to know that the message
of the portrait is a message from her, — from
Emilia Colonna.

IIer name sends through me a thrill deeper
than the thrill that came from her face alone,
when her name was still a secret. It arouses
again the thoughts that came to me when I
stood before the great Titian. Her life was
Magdalene's, with all its agony, and with no
sainthood to bless its end. I seem to see her
deep in the toils of sin, casting heavenward,
from her Roman palace, eyes that cannot
pierce the ceilings whence the painted gods
of the pagans grin down upon her with smiles
that the old Christians taught were the smiles
of Hell. I seem to see, too, the old Cardinal
in the midst of his prayer. Between them
there is an empty place. I press forward to
take it: and the rolling clouds gather about
me again, and I am in a great mist, moving

I know not whither. In God's name, let the light come!

. . . .

They have been haggling over the great Titian as if it were some trumpery trinket in a Roman shop,— the grinning Florentine, and the hard-faced Countess, and the sharp-voiced Yankee. I have bidden Cleveland take it from them. It shall be mine. To look at it gives me no delight; but when I look at it, thoughts come to me on which it is right that my mind should dwell. For me, for me alone, the old Venetian drew it unawares, three hundred years ago, and left it behind him, never dreaming of its mission. It shall not be dishonored by the barter of these hagglers.

. . . .

The great Titian is gone. It is best as it is, I suppose. That marvellous form will pass out of my life: if time will let it fade out of my memory too, I shall be the happier if not the better. Yet I am sick at heart when I think of the Magdalene, in all her old-world glory, spread

out before the eyes of the busy, trading world
that I have left behind me.   It is as if my heart
were opened to be stared at by the multitude.
It is as if all the secrets of my life, the riddles
that I myself cannot read, — the dead Duchess
and the old Cardinal, their nameless agonies and
mine, — were flung before the people for a show:
such a show the old Romans revelled in when
the wicked emperors ruled them.

.   .   .   .

There is no strength in me.   I was cured, I
thought, of the love I had felt for Filippa.   I
had fought out the fight within myself.   I was
content to leave her as I had found her, to look
upon her from afar off, to see her choose a fitting
mate from among the men who lived about her.
When I thought of the words of love that in
my presence she had whispered to the Count
Luigi, I felt my jealous sorrow no more.   " It is
best as it is," I said.   In my heart I blessed the
happiness which I dreamed was theirs.

For it was all a dream, — all save that she
may not be mine, that my fate bids me harden

my heart against all thoughts that are not of
the duty that shall be revealed to me when the
time shall come. She will never be his any
more than she shall be mine. She is betrothed,
betrothed to bald Palchi.

They make a grand ceremony of betrothal,
these Romans. I knew nothing of what was
doing until to-day, when once more I was making my way to the old Cardinal. I have said
no word to him of how I found him at his
prayer, of how I took the picture that strives
to show me how his life and mine are knit
together. But I have seen him many times;
and each time that I have come to his presence
I have felt more and more how foul a lie is that
which would whisper that he, who sheds about
him the blessing of holiness, wrought the sin
that makes the dead Emilia groan. Yet all
the same I have known that he could tell me
the secret that lies hidden in her painted eyes.
Each time that I have come to him, I have
come to beg that he would speak. Each time,
when I have found him in all his holiness, I

have shrunk from calling up any thought of evil things. In his presence I have been content to breathe the air of peace. Each time I have come from him with the words which I have had to say unspoken. Then each time I have called myself coward, and bidden myself gather courage to ask him the meaning of all.

To-day when his doors were opened to me, I heard an unwonted stir within; and found before me Monsignor dei Bardi, who seemed to be awaiting some guest. When he saw me he stepped forward, and told me with civil words that to-day I could not be admitted. A ceremony was about to take place, — the ceremony of betrothal; none but the kinsfolk of the couple were to be present.

I could not trust my ears; I muttered some half-foolish questions. Monsignor repeated what he had said: —

"I regret that I must ask you to withdraw. It has been stipulated that none but their relatives shall witness the betrothal of the Prince Palchi and the Contessina Filippa Barbarini."

Stupidly, hardly knowing what I did, I turned away ; and turning, found myself face to face with the dapper prince. He was coming in full dress, with three or four sparkling orders on his breast, to play his part in the ceremony. I bowed, and spoke words of formal congratulation. Not one of them was true. In an instant I was ashamed that I had spoken them.

" I am sensible of the honor of your felicitations," said the little prince, bowing until his bald head was half-way down to his varnished boots; " I am indeed the most fortunate of men."

And with that he passed within the doors, which closed behind him.

When I was left alone, I wanted air. I must breathe. I must gather my thoughts together. For the moment all things save Filippa had fled from my mind. I stumbled down the great stairway, hardly knowing where I trod. A man hastening upward was in my way. We stopped face to face. It was the Count Luigi. He was very pale. I looked at him for an instant in silence. His suffering, I thought, is more than mine. From him a life of glorious happiness is being snatched away. I have nothing to complain of save that my dreams are only dreams. I have slept, and thought myself a good spirit breathing blessings upon men; I wake to find that I am none. That is all. His is the real misery.

He looked at me as I looked at him. In his face I saw all the suffering that he felt. In mine I trust he saw the sympathy that filled my heart. I held him out my hand.

" They have told me what is passing," I said. "God be with you, friend."

He stood for a moment without a word. Then, of a sudden, he flung his arms about me and kissed my cheek.

" God bless you for your gentle word," he half sobbed. " You are worthy to be called a friend. You do not belong in this foul Old World of ours. You come from a land where men are men and not slaves, where life is life and not a prison."

Then, with another embrace, he was gone; and I was left alone. I heard the great doors close behind him. As I passed through the court-yard and out through the narrow street, I made my way among blazoned coaches and trampling horses that had borne their masters to the grand ceremony. And I wandered aimless through the Roman streets, while in the palace that I had left behind me Filippa was pledging her faith to the dapper prince.

. . . .

It must not be. It shall not be. Her life shall not be flung away upon such a man as her hard-faced mother has bidden her smile on. Her gallant lover shall not be cast aside. I will go to the Cardinal Giulio. He sits alone, his eyes fixed on Heaven, forgetting the world about him in his thoughts of the world to come. He knows not, in his holiness, what is done within his own doors. I will show him. A word from him shall cast down the evil edifice that they are rearing; for with all his holiness he is still the head of their house, and in that house

his word is law. I will go to him. He will speak
the word that shall free her. And then, on my
way through life, I shall have done one small
good deed; I shall not have waited idly for the
work that is preparing.

. . . .

I have seen him, alone again in the great room
which his presence had seemed to sanctify. I
am come away full of disquiet. I have built me
a house of dreams; a breath has cast it down.

He was alone, I say; and welcomed me with
as kind a smile as ever.

"It is good of you to come," he said; "you
always bring me happiness." And he held out
his blue-veined hand, on which, as had grown
my custom, I pressed my lips. Then for a little
while I was abashed and said nothing; but sat
still as I had sat with him before, full of confidence that he was good and faithful, sure that he
felt a like confidence in me. A woman might
sit so with her lover.

Finally I gathered up my courage, and asked
him if he knew what was done yesterday.

" Surely," he said, " yesterday was a happy day in the history of my family. An alliance was made that will do us much honor."

I looked at him amazed. His face was calm ; it wore a look of content, a smile ; but the smile was not like those that I was used to see on his lips. There was something in it that called up before me the smile of the tricky Florentine ; nay, that even seemed to know the secret of the mirth with which the carven satyrs writhed on his great chair.

" Indeed," he went on, " the alliance was of my making. It was no easy work. In such matters complications come which one who has led a simple life like yours can hardly imagine. To have reached this happy conclusion gives me great satisfaction. There are few worldly things left to trouble me now."

Had I been wrong ? I wondered. Had my fancy conjured up a tragedy when really all things went well ?

" Does she love him, then ? " I asked, so abruptly that I started at the rudeness of my voice.

" Surely not now," said the old Cardinal, with a look of surprise. " What should a young girl, well brought up, know of love ? "

" And you have let her promise herself without love ! " I cried, full of amazement that he, who had seemed to me all goodness, looked with no frown upon this evil.

" We have bidden her do what seemed best to those who were most fitted to judge of her welfare," he answered, with a dignity that had in it some shade of reproof; for what I said seemed to him, I think, meddlesome. " She has obeyed with dutiful readiness."

With that he spoke some other words, of commonplace matters, to show me, I suppose, that we had said enough of this. But a spirit was aroused within me that would not be silenced. I broke out with many words, asking him what good could come of a match like this ; what manner of life would be theirs, who were bound together by formal words and by no closer bond.

He looked at me with displeasure. His face

grew severe; it flushed as if with anger; for the first time I saw it lose the paleness of age. Such life would be theirs, he said with growing sternness, as had been the life of their fathers before them, as had been the life of their people for generations. Marriage must be, that the race of men may be perpetuated on the earth; and so God through the Church has sanctified it. But marriage should be kept free from carnal lust; human creatures who grow to love one another too much lose sight of the higher things toward which they ought always to look. And so a marriage like this, made by thoughtful friends who know what is best, is a purer thing, and a holier, than the sanctified amour which I seemed to think the true one. Such plans as his bind bodies alone together, and leave husband and wife soul-free to fulfil the aspirations that arise within them. Such thoughts as mine desecrate the sacrament.

As he spoke, my hand had wandered about my breast, and had fallen upon the miniature of Emilia Colonna, which I carried there. I drew it forth, urged by an impulse of which I had small consciousness. When his voice ceased, his eye was fixed upon me, full of the displeasure that had led him to rebuke me with all the authority of the Church ; and he drew a deep breath, like one who has spoken things that may not be answered.

I made no answer ; but laid the portrait before him, asking him whose face it showed.

The flush left his face as he bent down his head and looked at what I showed him. I thought that he would have fainted, for he trembled so that I could see his hands quiver, as they tried to grasp the arms of his chair and hold themselves firm. But he set his lips, and kept his voice calm.

"It is Emilia, my brother's wife," he said. "How came it to you?"

"What manner of life was hers?" I asked him solemnly.

He stretched out his hand, and took the picture, and held it close to his dull eyes.

"I prayed Heaven that I might see her face

no more," he said, as if he knew not that I was by. " When I arose from my prayer her face was gone ; and I troubled myself not to know how it was gone, for my prayer was granted. And now it comes again, to drag me back to the evil days of old, with its witch's eyes, with its devil's smile. I will look on it no more. No man shall look on it again."

With that he stretched out his arm as if to lay the face of the portrait upon the table by his side, but stopped half-way, and brought it back before his eyes ; and I could see that his thin fingers clutched it so tightly that the fretted frame cut them deep. Then, of a sudden, he raised it and kissed it as he might have kissed the lips it mimicked. But when he felt its touch he started as if from a poisoned sting ; and with a great effort he flung it from him, and it fell and was shattered to pieces on the marble floor. Then he leaned back in his great chair, and closed his eyes ; and his pale face was like the face of a dead man whose last moments knew no peace.

What made me speak, I know not; but I spoke again, startled to hear my own voice.

" What manner of life was hers?" I heard myself say once more, — " hers, whose marriage was such as you would make Filippa's? What blessing, what purity of spirit came to her from the union that your Church had blest? Would you have Filippa live as in the olden time Emilia Colonna lived?"

The old Cardinal had started up. Resting his hands upon the arms of his great chair, he had raised himself to his feet. He stood before me, holding himself firm upon the limbs that in common times could hardly bear his weight. He raised himself up until he stood erect, and in his sweeping robes looked taller than common men.

"Stop!" he cried, lifting his hand with a gesture of command. "No man speaks her name to me! I have cherished you because in you I found a memory of what she was, purged of the old sins that clung to her life and mine. It was a new sin, — a devil's snare. Leave me! Come to me no more!"

I stood abashed. I knew not what I should do.

" Leave me ! " he cried again ; and he moved his hand with a passionate gesture, as if he would sweep me away like some evil thing.

Then I stammered words that should deprecate his anger. But interrupting, he bade me leave him, more firmly than before. So, full of trouble, I turned away. And as I went I heard his slow steps tottering toward the great crucifix where I had seen him at his prayer.

.   .   .   .

And this, men would tell me, should be the end of all. My life has touched the life of another, greater by far than I. My eyes have been dazzled with his greatness ; he has seemed to me all pure and good. He has deigned to let me approach him for a while ; and I, grown overbold, have presumed too much. Then he has cast me out with no gentle words, showing himself other than I thought him. He has spoken the language of this Old World, whose corruptions we of the New cast off when our fathers crossed the stormy seas to plant themselves in the forests that knew no evil. I have dreamed a dream, men would tell me. I should rub my eyes and awake.

I would that I could do their bidding; but it may not be. The bonds that bind me to Giulio Colonna may not be broken thus. What they are I cannot tell. Whither his life and mine shall be carried together I cannot see. But the old knowledge that came to me when I saw him first is no whit less clear than before. The work for which I was born, the work toward which I have travelled even as the wise men of old travelled toward the star of which they knew not the meaning, is a work that has to do with him in his dark palace, and with the dead Duchess, whose eyes gaze at me still in memory as they gazed yesterday from the image that lies shivered at his feet.

Yes, we are bound together, I know not how; we are bound as lovers might be bound, by a common fate which lies beyond our ken. The time shall come, in some other world if not in this, when Giulio Colonna and I shall cling together, shall move together through the eternities, working out the destinies for which we were born. But it shall not be as it has seemed to me before. He shall not be my leader. Nay, I shall rather be his, for we are fallen on evil times, and of their evil I know as much as he; and the impulse that comes to me now bids me forget his angry words, and hold out my hand, and lead him forth from sinful Rome, full of the whoredoms of the ages, to the light of God, which gleams through the clouds that writhe about me as I struggle on alone.

Let the light come! Let it come quickly!

X.

From Beverly's Journal.

TO-NIGHT, when I was alone, there came a hasty knock at my door. I went to answer it. Before me stood a man wrapped in a cloak. I could not see his face; I lifted my candle above my head and peered at him in the darkness.

"It is you," he said; "I am glad." I knew his voice. He was the Count Luigi Orsini. He glided in with a stealthy step, and closed the door very quietly. Then he turned to me again, flinging back his dark cloak.

"I am glad that you are here alone," he said. "You alone spoke words of comfort to me on that day when they were tearing out my heart. To you alone I must say farewell."

For a moment I thought that he meant to take his life, to snatch if he could in another

world the peace his kinsfolk have stolen from
him in this. I knew not what to say. I stood
looking at him full of uneasiness. But he met
my gaze with a fearless eye, with a smile of
courage, not of despair.

"You are an American," he said; "I can
trust you. You come from a land where men
are free, where life has broken its shackles.
You are grown so used to freedom that you
do not know its worth. We know it here.
Freedom has not dwelt in Italy for a thousand
years. All the men of your great continent
are brothers; they are called by a common
name, which thrills them when they hear it
spoken. Here there are no Italians; we may
not speak that word. We are Romans or Flor-
entines or Neapolitans; we must bow down
before one or another of the little princes and
priests who are tearing the entrails of Italy.
That is a noble destiny to be born to!"

He stopped speaking. All his meaning, I
think, could not have come to me; for the
charm that Italy had cast upon me rose strong

in my mind; and I began to speak of the
beauty of his country, to tell him how it had
found an empty place in my heart and filled
it.

" Yes," he said, " Italy has lovers. She has
always had them. Such beauty as hers cannot
fail of love. But her lovers are like the lovers
of a harlot. They breathe their passion only for
their pleasure; and when their love is sated,
they fling her money, and leave her to her fate.
Well! it is over with me now. I have cast
away the mask. I leave Rome to-night. If I
stayed it would be in a prison."

Even then I did not understand him ; and
asked him what was his crime, fearing that in
his passion he had done some evil thing.

" I have dared to be an Italian as you are
an American," he said. And then he told his
story as we sat together in my room, where the
dim candle-light made the walls look vaster than
structures reared by human hands.

The men in Rome are not few who feel as he
has spoken to-night. If they speak aloud they

are flung into prison ; there they die in silence.
So they meet by stealth, and plan in secret for a
time when Italy shall at last be Italy, — a time
which they hope is at hand. For months his
life has been one that no man can lead with
safety, though each who leads it hopes that he
may escape the suspicion which must stop his
work for the cause he loves. Soon or late, each
man's time comes at last. The Count Luigi's
time was come to-night. Monsignor dei Bardi
had sent for him.

"That black serpent glides everywhere," said
the Count; "when I saw his scowling face I
knew what was coming. He hopes, you know,
that the Cardinal Colonna will be made pope.
You have seen how he mákes the old man play
the dying saint, as Sixtus and Leo the Twelfth
played it before him. When Capellari[1] sickens,
Monsignor will give the viaticum to the Cardinal Giulio. Then he will bring him back by a
miracle to a feeble life that shall tickle the
ambition of the conclave. If the Cardinal Giulio

[1] Gregory XVI.

is made pope, Monsignor will come to him and
say, ' Do by me as I have done by you.' Then
he will be made cardinal; and who knows what
may come after that? All his sly life is spent
in wriggling toward the red hat that he is trying to put in the Cardinal Giulio's gift. And
I, he finds, — a near friend of His Eminence,
almost a member of his household, — am play-
ing at games that are forbidden."

Then he went on to tell how Monsignor had
stormed and threatened, trying to make him
tell the secrets of his friends. If he would
speak out, the priest promised, he should have
safety and honors ; for the Pope knows how
to reward his friends, let them be faithless as
devils to all other ties. He is the Vicegerent
of God ; to serve him is to serve Heaven, to
play his foes false is to confound the children
of Hell. And those who do his pleasure on
this earth, let it lead them where it may, are
sure of seats among the saints. So Monsignor stood in his black robes, and stamped his
buckled shoes, and grumbled forth the distant

thunders of the Church that might be launched upon the heads of those who would not do his bidding, and promised rewards in this world and in the next to those who would bend their will to his. And the Count Luigi stood before him and listened, making no answer.

For at first he was tempted to break out with answering reproaches, to speak as he had spoken to me of the miseries of Italy, of the sins of the priestcraft that has ground her in the dust for a thousand years. But in a moment came wiser counsels, and he held his peace. Nothing could come from a war of words save the clashing of the prison doors that should shut him out from the world as they had shut out his friends before him. So he stood listening to threats and to promises. And the priest thought from his silence that he was ready to speak; and seizing a pen bade him say out the words that should save him and dash to pieces the plans his friends cherished with their lives.

Then danger gave the Count counsels that he had not deemed himself wise enough to hold.

In the subtle world where he has lived he has learned the secret of trickery; he can speak with a smooth face words that tell nothing of the thoughts that lie behind them. To-night this skill stood him in good stead. With well-counterfeited terror and contrition he told Monsignor a long tale of secrets that he knew and of secrets that were hidden from him ; and he told his tale so well that the priest believed he spoke the truth. Then he spoke to the tricky churchman of the dangers that would beset him if his faithlessness were known before he had time to seek safety ; and he pledged the priest to act slowly and secretly; and at last had leave to go. So he went, having said no word that could harm his friends, and having gained time.

He hurried to his friends, and warned them that the time was over when they could stay in peace at Rome. For months their plans had been making to slip away, and in secret places not far off to plan a great onset on the powers that tear asunder Italy. In an hour all was settled. Even now, while I write these lines, they are spurring away from Rome. Whither they are going I know as little as any; but I know that in good time they shall come again, bearing with them, in spite of priests and priest-craft, the Italian fatherland that the poets and the seers have longed for.

Then, when there were few moments left, he bethought him of me, and of how I alone of all who knew him had shown him that I cared for what he felt when Filippa pledged her faith to Palchi. Full of confidence that I, a free American, should care too for the love of country that exiled him from his home, that I should not betray him, he was come to press my hand once more, to whisper one more word of gratitude for the word of kindness that I had spoken.

I could not understand all this. The simple words he spoke so frankly were not so vital that it was worth his while to come and speak them here; for if he were found in the Colonna palace he would be dragged away to prison.

Still, though I wondered greatly, this seemed no time to speak of my wonder. So I took his hands and pressed them, and bade him God-speed. And then I thought he would go.

But he stood still, hesitating for a moment. Then, of a sudden, he took a ring from his finger and placed it in my hand.

"It is for her," he said, "for Filippa. I must go without a word. I cannot go and leave no token. No one will suspect you, who pass in and out of the Cardinal Giulio's home. Give her this when chance allows you. Whisper as you give it that I love her still; that I will come again; that her name shall be on my lips through every waking hour; that her face shall be in all my dreams. Tell her how I pray that mine may sometimes be in hers."

I held the ring. I had almost said that I would be the messenger of his love. But of a sudden, before I had spoken any word, there came to me the knowledge of what this mission meant. She was pledged to another; the love of which I could bear the message was no holy love. I bit my lip that would have spoken. I gave him back his ring, saying that I could not do as he would have me, when she to whom he sent his greeting could never be his wife.

He looked at me as if he did not understand.

" Her lips have promised her to Palchi," he said ; " her heart is mine. You know it as well as I."

Then I told him that the heart might not go without sin where the lips had promised that it should not ; and that I would be the go-between of no unrighteous love. Interrupting me, he burst out in a storm of passion, swearing that I was no true friend. And when he saw that I could not be moved, he stamped his foot, and uttered wild curses, and turned and fled away and left me.

So all these things that I have let myself love are false. The beauty of this Italy whose heart is here by the yellow Tiber — the beauty that filled me with a great happiness when first it glowed before me at the foot of the cold Alps — is a devil's beauty. It covers things hideous,

unspeakable. The joy it brings is like the joy
that lurks in the wine-cup. It is charged with
evil; and when we have drunk our fill, there
comes a great loathing of what we have done.
To-night I would shake the dust of Rome from
my feet, and fly to some land where I may
breathe pure air. But it may not be. The
voice within me whose warnings I may not set
aside tells me that here, in the midst of guile,
I must linger on until I know at last why I am
come hither, whither my footsteps must take
their way. So I linger still, sick at heart, waiting for the light that shall guide me on.

And now I shall break away from Beverly
for a while, and tell a part of the story in my
own words again.

XI

IN the midst of Rome there stands an old
church, not large and not so fine as most
of those that have famous names. But the low
round arches, and the dim mosaics that peer
down with big eyes from the Tribune in the
midst of which Christ blesses the people, show
that it belongs to the oldest of Christian days.
Legend says that it was built to keep alive the
memory of a Roman virgin who suffered martyr-
dom on the spot where it stands. Emilia, the
legend runs, was the daughter of a great noble-
man who hated the Christians as bitterly as did
the emperor himself. Her father bade her marry
an officer of the court, famous for the cruelty
with which he hunted down those of the new
faith ; and preparations were making for a grand
wedding.. But a Christian slave who was in
attendance on the maiden converted her to the

truth. So when the wedding-day came she would be the bride of none but Christ. In a rage her father struck her down; and folding her hands, and muttering a last prayer for him, she died. In later times, when the Christians had risen above persecution and ruled the city, the holy martyr Emilia appeared in a vision to a priest; and showing him the spot where the house had stood in which she had met her death, she bade him build a church there. So the church was built; and then, by another miracle, they found somewhere in the Catacombs the body of Santa Emilia, which they placed with solemn rejoicing upon the high altar of the church. And thither for a thousand years men have come to worship.

In this church the Colonnas were buried, at first simply enough, in tombs that no man could envy save for their quietness. But by and by a rich member of the house, stirred by the magnificence with which some rival families decked their burial-places, built beside the little church a grand chapel blazing with strange marbles

that had been dug up among the ruins of pagan
Rome. In this chapel the Colonnas lie now,
and among them the Duchess Emilia.

Elsewhere than in Rome, this old church —
sweet with the incense of centuries, and splen-
did, too, since the door that leads to the princely
chapel has been opened in its gray wall — would
be a famous spot. But in Rome, over-rich with
treasures of art and of tradition, it stands un-
noticed. Indeed, when I went to Rome, years
after Beverly was dead and forgotten, I had
much work to find it. The local guides and the
grand porter of my hotel had never heard its
name. "It is possible that there is such a
place," they would say; "but who cares to go
there?" All the same I sought it out, and
found there many a quiet thought of past time.
Such thoughts have come to me in the dead old
towns of New England, whose wooden mansions
will have rotted away for centuries before a
stone falls from the mosaics of Santa Emilia.
The world has passed it by. None but the
Colonnas remember it, if indeed there are still

10

Colonnas in Rome. For I put no questions to the snuffy *custode* who unlocked for me the iron gate of their chapel; I only passed within it, and stood among the marbles whose splendor seemed strangely out of keeping with the solemnity of death. We of New England think of the dead in quiet church-yards, where gray stone slabs, half overgrown with moss, stand amid the long grass. There rude rhymes sing their dirges in quaintly simple tones that lose themselves in the low harmonies of the wind which plays through the slow-moving branches of elms and pines. In Rome the spirit of the old pagans is not dead. As they strove to make bright the homes of their departed with dancing sprites and merry colors, so the Romans even in our own time deck their graves with such splendors as they love in life.

In the Colonna chapel there is a monument made by some follower of Canova, and on it is the name of the Duchess Emilia. I stood before it, thinking of the time — not far off in years, yet so far in all things else — when

Richard Beverly had found his way there too. For there Beverly came, by mere chance; and there at last was revealed to him what he believed with all his heart to be the secret of his life.

It was not long after the time of which he wrote in the last lines I have copied from his journal. Cut off by what seemed a cruel fate rather than any fault of his from all the friends who were near him, — from the Clevelands, from the old Cardinal Colonna, from the Count Luigi, from Filippa, whom he still calls Filippa in his writing, — he wandered about the city, seeking distraction from himself. His journal contains many notes, such as all travellers make, of sights that have been written of a thousand times and will be written of as long as Rome lasts. At length, he found himself one day before the little church of Santa Emilia, and entered to see what might be within. There he found just such an old *custode* as met me there years afterwards, — perhaps the same, for the man I saw looked old enough to have been there

since the days of the blessed Emilia herself.
And this old creature told him, in a cracked
voice that he noted in his journal, the simple
story of the saint ; and showed him the shrine
that holds her bones. So he stood before the
shrine, studded with jewels which look very
like bits of polished glass, and thought of what
her life had been who lies on earth, as she sits
in Heaven, in glory. Nothing could be simpler
or slighter. A young girl, faithful to the God
whom she had learned to worship, would not
swerve from what she thought He bade her do.
Pure He had made her ; pure she would give
herself back to Him. So she died, and might
have been forgotten, but that the Roman Christians have never suffered simple purity to die.
What good has come within their ken they have
gathered up and treasured. They have decked
it, perhaps, in such feeble poetry as is made
only in monkish minds ; they have shrined its
relics in cases that make sane men smile. But
all the same they have treasured it. The church
that has bred all the subtleties of Roman priest-

craft is the church that has kept alive the memory of the saints and the martyrs who gave themselves with all their hearts to what they deemed was the truth.

Some such thoughts came to Beverly, as he stood before the shrine of the Roman girl who has outlived the great world that did her to death. But he was not suffered to think of her long. The old *custode*, hungry for another fee, dragged him off to the chapel, — more beautiful, the *custode* said, than Paradise itself, — which was the glory of this old church; and unlocked the iron gate, which creaked on its hinges, and forced him to enter. What he found there he shall tell in his own words.

From Beverly's Journal.

As I stepped within the chapel there came to me more strongly than ever the feeling that I was moving through a world where I had been before. And this old feeling came in a form which I had not yet known. Before, it had been as if I was come back from afar off

to spots full of evil memories too vague and distant for me to know what they were. Here at
last it was as if I was come face to face with
the evil thing that has chased me through my
life. I half thought that some shadowy form
would stalk before me, and whisper in my ear
words that should bear their meaning to my
heart. But nothing came; and I smiled at
my folly as I looked about me at the marble
splendors which the cracked-voiced verger
pointed out.

Where I was I did not know; I had not
stopped to ask. Whose tombs I looked at I
hardly cared. I would have turned back and
left the spot, trusting that the evil thoughts
which came to me there were only the delusions
of a troubled mind. In truth, it seems to me
that I did turn back, bidding my old guide
show me no more. But of that I know little;
for, as I turned, my eyes fell upon a thing that
in my earthly life I had never seen before.
And then, for a long time, I saw and knew
nothing of what was done about me. But I

saw and knew instead the things for which I had strained my mind so long.

For there before me on a sculptured tomb was the name that had echoed through my brain when Cleveland spoke it, the name that the old Cardinal had bidden me never speak to him, — Emilia Colonna. I saw no other word save the date when she died. It was my birth-year. That I had known. But as I looked upon the letters I read more, which had never been told me. It was on the very day when I was born in far-off New England that Emilia Colonna came to her end in Rome. Her life went out of the world as mine came into it. A simple fact enough, men might say; but to me it had a meaning that unlocked the riddle of my life. Not all at once did the truth come to me, but all at once I knew that it was coming; and I stood leaning against the sculptured marble, my eyes fixed upon the formal words, as the truth that I had sought came shining through the murky clouds of mystery that have writhed about me so long. It .

shone through at last, as the sun shines through
a mountain mist, — first faint and dim, then
more and more distinct, at last in all the clear-
ness of heaven. But the truth that came to
me had little of heaven in it.

For at first there swept over me memories
of her sinful life whose bones lay within the
marble tomb. I thought of her loveless marriage, of her unhallowed love. I thought of
how Duke Pietro, whose tomb was by hers, had
fallen murdered before her tearless eyes; of
how, while he lay dead, she had sat in her palace waiting for the lover who had dishonored
the dead man's name. I thought of how from
that day on no touch of penitence had come to
her proud spirit; of how she had sunk deep in
all the sins of the flesh, smiling, with the lips
I had known for mine in the painted face she
left behind her, on every lover who pressed
his suit. And then at last she had died in the
midst of her sin; and they had brought her
hither and laid her beside her honest lord, to
sleep in peace.

Here she had been, in her marble bed, since the day when I first drew breath in this world. That was strange, — that I, whose simple life was not begun until her stormy life was ended, should be standing by her tomb, telling over the tale of her sins as a monk might tell the beads of his rosary. Nay, I was telling them as if they had been part of my own life, the life that was not yet in being when those sins were done. For with each thought of what her sins had been there came to me a fresh pang. I shrunk from them, as I would have shrunk if I had done them in my own flesh. Yet from them I could not shrink away, even as I could never shrink away from myself.

What all meant I could not tell ; but I saw that the truth was at hand. I fell upon my knees, crying out to Heaven in my own tongue that I might be kept in the dark no longer. Vile as I was, let me see the light, and I would struggle toward it with all the might that was in me.

Then my eyes were cleared once more. It

was as if some hand had swept away the veil
of mystery which had hidden from me the place
in which I stood ; for in my misery I had ceased
to see, to hear, to feel. And when I knew that
my eyes could see once more, I found them fixed
upon the words which told me that here before
me lay the dead woman, who died on the day
when I was born.

With that came to me the memory of an old
tale that my nurse told me when I was a little
child. It was in the midst of a stormy night
that I came into the world. When I was born
I was still and lifeless, and they said that
there was no earthly life for me, that I was
dead in the womb. But of a sudden, as the
clocks were tolling the hour of midnight, I
quivered and uttered a great cry, louder and
wilder than the cries of other children. And
I drew breath with a struggle, as if I would
fain lie still but could not ; and cried again
with a voice of fear that made the women
start. Then I lived ; and living I was come
back here at last.

For from hence I was come. The mystery was clear to me now. The life that has filled my waking hours with agony was come from hence. The spirit that brought life to the baby form that might have lain at peace among my fathers was no blessed sprite from Heaven. But in the stormy midnight the soul that had been Emilia's was whirled about the rolling earth; and coming to my far-off fatherland it found a wretched home in the madman's body that is mine. Saved for a time by what blessed power no man can tell from the fires of Hell, it lingers on in this earth with one more chance to expiate its sin.

All the mystery that I have found in Rome was cleared. All the agony that I have suffered was real and true, a thousand-fold more than I had dreamed. I knelt, and prayed with all my heart for light and for mercy. And as I raised my living hands to God, it seemed to me that the dead hands which had been mine raised themselves too within the tomb. Then presently I knew no more.

When my life came back to me, I was lying in the sacristy of the old church ; and they were bathing my temples with cool water. Before long I raised myself up, stronger and calmer than I had been in the time gone by. And I gave them money, and came my way hither to my chamber in the old palace.

Here I wait to-night, full of agony deeper than I knew of old, for now the sins for which I suffer are as clear to me as they are to the Heaven by whose justice the suffering has followed them. But I am full of hope, too, that the mercy which has saved me to this time will not forsake me now; that it will lead me on through agonies of expiation as great as souls can bear, until at last the sin is washed away. Then shall come rest, rest such as God alone can grant.

XII.

SO this was the secret which Beverly had been seeking so long. It seems a mad thought; no doubt it was. My friends will look at me askance and whisper predictions of a time when I shall be locked up at Somerville if I venture to breathe that there are moments when I see in it something besides madness. But, mad or not, this thought, which to Beverly was the deepest he ever knew, struck a note that brought into harmony all the restless discords of his life. And in that harmony, fantastic as it is, I have grown to find a beauty that is not quite of this world. So it seemed to Beverly when his last hour came. So, when the end was come, it seemed to the old Cardinal Colonna. And we three are all that have pondered on the story until it has become part of our lives.

From the time when Beverly saw the church
of Santa Emilia, his life moved swiftly and surely
to its end. Day after day he lived on, waiting
for the revelation of his duty. Day after day
he went from the quiet rooms where now he
lived all alone to the little church ; and there,
flinging a piece of silver to the old *custode,* he
passed into the chapel of the Colonnas, and
knelt by the tomb that held Emilia Colonna's
bones, and prayed. Again and again he told
over in his mind the story of her sins. More
and more he grew to feel that those sins were
upon his soul, that all the misery which he had
suffered, he had not known why, was mercy
by the side of what those sins deserved. And
though the suffering that he felt now was keener
than the vague pangs he had felt before, it
troubled him less, for now he knew what it
meant and why it came.

"There is one thought," he writes, "which
gives me comfort. In all the life that I have
lived since I have been the being that I am
to-day, I have done with all my heart what I

thought was right. I have idled, perhaps; I
have not looked about me. But when tempta-
tions have come, I have struggled against them;
when a duty has lain before me, I have striven
to do it. So with God's help I will persist."

One day, when he came near the church, he
found the streets astir; and asking of some one
in the crowd why they had gathered, was told
that this was the festival of Santa Emilia. There
was a grand service in the little church; there
was to be a procession through the streets of
the parish; and so many dark-eyed Romans
were come together to see the solemnities that
he found it no easy matter to make his way to
a spot whence the rough brick wall of the church
was in sight. The rest of what happened this
day he shall tell for himself: —

From Beverly's Journal.

So great was the crowd gathered at the church
door that I gave up all thought of entering, and
stood among them waiting to see what might
come. Through the open doors, whence came

the sound of organ music, I could catch a glimpse of the altar, sparkling with great candles and with colored lamps, which shone amid clouds of incense-smoke as stars shine through evening mists. Before long the organ music ceased, and there was a little lull, so that I could hear the people talking of the sight that was coming. Then, of a sudden, when I was not prepared for it, came a burst of song from the church, as if the whole company within were one great choir. The crowd about the doors parted ; some fell on their knees ; and the procession came forth singing a glorious hymn. First in the hymn came a song of solemn triumph, and in this all the voices joined. Then came a passage which the choir boys sang cheerily, as if their hearts were glad ; the music was sweet and simple, and flowed as if it were not studied, but came of itself to the singers. Then came again the great chorus of triumph. So the procession passed out of the church, with a cross at its head, and made its way through the crowded streets.

There were priests in robes of many kinds,

and there were boys who sang as if all their lives
were one long song, and others who swung
censers, from which the smoke curled up and
filled the air with fragrance ; and there were
great crosses and banners, and finally a reli-
quary in which lay some of the bones that they
say were hers in whose honor all these things
were done. So, with joyous song, this holy
company made their way among the people.
And the people watched them happily, thinking
of the girl whose pure life ended here in pain
and sorrow near two thousand years ago. She
was true to her God. Undefiled He made her ;
undefiled she gave herself to Him. That faithful deed is deemed worthy to keep her memory
alive through the ages ; from year to year they
sing her praises in such grand hymns as I have
heard to-day. So through all time the people
remember her who gave little thought to herself, and they bless her memory, praying that
she may bring her purity before the throne of
God, to beg His mercy for them ; for one good
life, they say, is more grateful to Heaven than

a thousand evil ones are hateful, — such is the mercy of God.

When the joyous procession was past, the crowd was less dense. So I made my way toward the church, and at last passed up the steps and within the doors. There the light was dim; so I stood still for a while that my eyes might grow used to it; and as the people were pressing about me I stepped aside and stood by the wall close to the door. Near me was a woman whose face was veiled. When she saw me she drew her veil closer, as if she thought that I would look at her rudely. What she was like I could not tell; she might be young or old, fair or ugly, for her dress was very plain and her veil hid her face. She gave only one glance to me. Then she looked about her, as if she waited for some one who did not come.

As the crowd surged about the doorway, there approached her a fellow in the dress of the people. He looked like any other. Until he was close to her she did not remark him; but when he was at her side he spoke in a whisper some word which made her start. I could see her clasp his hand and hold it fast as she whispered back. It was he for whom she had been waiting here, for whom she had turned this feast of purity into a masque of love. And her love, I thought, could be no true one, else why should it hide itself behind veils and disguises? For, whoever she was, she was no woman of the people, and the man she met could not be the peasant that he seemed. His face was turned from me. I could see only his thick black hair, and his bearded cheek, and the passion which burst through all his efforts to control it, as he spoke to her who was come to meet him.

It was strange. There was about this man and this woman something that I had known before, — not in the mysterious way in which I have known the Roman things that in my present life met my eyes for the first time, but firmly, really, as I had known Cleveland, and the old Cardinal Colonna, and Filippa.

Then of a sudden the man turned his face;

and in spite of his beard and of his strange dress
I knew him for the Count Luigi. And then I
knew that the woman he spoke with was Filippa
herself. Yes, here — in the shadow of the tomb
of Emilia Colonna, in the midst of the music that
sang the praises of the virgin saint, before my
eyes who drag out the miserable life of expiation that I call mine — they were come to whisper secret vows, to begin afresh such work as
wrought the agony that I suffer day and night.
I could not keep myself back. I laid my hand
upon their clasped hands ; and as they looked
at me in anger and in wonder I parted them
and stood between them.

" Count Luigi," I said, in a voice so low that
no one of the crowd about us knew that I spoke,
" this is no good deed. Contessina, come with
me."

In any other spot he would have struck me
down, and she too would have stabbed me with
her hands as she did now with the marvellous
eyes that flashed between the folds of her
veil. But here and now the danger was too

great. Even here he turned upon me; and putting his lips close to my ear poured out a torrent of evil words, calling down upon me all the miseries that his fancy could conjure up, as if my misery were not already beyond thought of men.

"Go," I said to him, "or I will call your name and give you up."

"Go," said Filippa then. "This madman shall do me no harm; and a word from him may destroy you. Go, for my sake."

"Lowest of scoundrels!" hissed Luigi in my ear, "you shall curse this day."

"With God's help," I said, "I will make you bless it."

Then I took Filippa's arm and drew it within my own, and forced her to move with me into the crowd that was about us. There the Count Luigi could not follow. So he went his way, I know not whither, to safety.

Filippa's hand grasped my arm as if she would crush it. She looked at me as her fingers tightened.

"I wish it were your black heart," she whispered; "then I could squeeze it to death."

"Contessina," I said very gently, "I wish you nothing but good. Come with me a little way."

"Where would you have me go?" she asked. "Do you think that I will follow you through eternity?"

"God forbid!" said I, and I felt myself tremble as I thought what her words might mean; it was to save her from that very fate that I dared to do what I did now. "I shall lead you only a little way. Then you shall go in peace."

I led her, quivering with anger and with fear lest some should know her, or I should do some strange thing, through the festal crowd until we came to the gate of the Colonna chapel. The gate was closed, but when I laid my hand upon it I found that it yielded to the pressure. By chance, the lock was not fast.

"It is here that I am leading you," I said; "here I can speak to you best." And I led her within ; and we stood together among the glowing marbles of old Rome, before Emilia Colonna's tomb.

As I looked toward the tomb I saw with wonder that one was there before us, but so lost in thought that he did not heed our coming. Alone before the sculptured tomb, gazing upon the lines that told who lay within it, stood a black-robed priest. His rusty dress seemed to show his poverty ; but in spite of his garb and of his loneliness I knew him for one whom I had never thought to see save in the grandeur of the state that was truly his. For it was the Cardinal Giulio Colonna, come in secret on the feast of her who had been dearest to him of human things, to watch before the tomb that held within it her bones, to pray perhaps that the soul which had been hers might find mercy in the sight of God, to whose service he had given his life.

As I looked on him there came to me feelings that were new and old at once. I thought how in the far-off time, when his step had been firm and his eye full of the fire of youth, he had whispered the passion of his heart to Emilia Colonna; how he had clasped her hands in his, and pressed her to his bosom with warm kisses. And as I thought of that love, treacherous in the sight of God and men, yet loyal in itself, constant, in spite of fastings and of prayers, through the long years that stretched on between the days when it was young and the time when he too should lay himself to rest among these Roman marbles, I felt my heart swell with answering love, strong and deep as a woman might give her lover. For a moment this was all that I felt; I would have stepped forward and spoken it out, had not the girl I had brought thither called me back to what I am.

" Why have you brought me here ? " she asked, in no steady voice, for the solemnity of the place had touched her with fear.

I pointed to the tomb of Emilia Colonna.

" To save you," I said, " from such a fate as hers. To save your spirit from the agony of a sin that may never be undone. To help you,

with God's help, so to live your earthly life that
when the end shall come you may rest in His
peace. Remember her. Remember me, too.
Perhaps the time may come when your prayers
shall help to win me mercy."

With that I motioned her away; and with
wondering eyes she went, moved deeply by the
strangeness of what I said. So I was left alone
with Giulio Colonna, who knew not yet that
any one was near him.

He stood still, his eyes fixed on the marble
tomb of Emilia, his lips moving as if in prayer.
Was his thought, I wondered, there in the
chapel of his fathers? Or did it wander into
the future, where his old life must soon merge
in the mysteries that lie beyond the grave? Or
did he think of her from whom he had parted
in the olden time, and wonder where the life that
had been hers dragged out the agony that justice should have meted it for all the eternities?
Or perchance did his thoughts wander back
to that olden time, when in blissful sin those
charms were his which now lay mouldering?

What love had been his for the woman whom human law and law divine had bidden him look at with no loving eyes! What love had been hers for him, in all the beauty of the youth that he had given her, in spite of earth and Heaven! Even now it seemed that, purged of earthliness, I felt that love still. The agonies that had been mine were not mine alone. Parted from me by half a world and by all the mystery of the being that I call mine, Giulio Colonna had felt them too, had shared them, not knowing that they were shared. The thought made them lighter. In sorrow there is ever a sad joy in knowing that others know the sorrow that bows us down.

"Giulio!" I found myself murmuring of him whom in this life I have known only as the prince of a church that is not mine. Yes, to me as I stood there he was Giulio still,—the dark-eyed boy who loved me in old Rome.

"Giulio!" I murmured again.

He heard me. He started, as if my voice had come from the tomb. Quickly, as if he were

still young, his hand made the sign of the cross.
He turned about, his face full of amazement.
He thought, I believe, to see before him some
being of another world.

"In God's name, who speaks to me?" he
cried aloud.

But when he saw me he knew me only for
the man whom he had driven from his presence.
His face grew stern with displeasure; he strove
to speak with a firm voice, to stand with a firm
footing.

"You have no right here, rude fellow," he
said; but as he spoke his voice faltered, and
he trembled and would have fallen.

Then I reached out my arms and held him
up, and looked at the old face that knew not
that I had known it when it was not old. And
in his weakness, half-wondering, half-angry, he
could not but lean upon me. So for a moment
I clasped him in my arms.

Then, when I might have spoken out the
secret of which my heart was full, there came to
my ears the swelling sound of the hymn that

the people were singing in honor of the virgin
saint. And I remembered in whose temple we
stood ; and with that memory came the thought
of what manner of life had been hers who bore
in later time the virgin Emilia's name. I shrank
away from the man who had soiled her life
when still it was pure. Yet I could not fling
him from me. So, very gently I laid him down
upon the marble steps of the altar that stood
in the chapel. And he sat trembling, looking
at me in wonder.

So I left him, alone in the chapel of his
fathers. And as I passed out into the church,
I found the people rejoicing once more; and
through the entrance doors came to meet me
the crosses and the banners and the smoking
censers of the company that had sung through
the streets of Rome hosannas to the virgin
saint.

XIII.

WHEN the Cardinal Colonna bade me come to him again I could not choose but go ; for perhaps through him, in some way that I could not foresee, might come the revelation of my duty, whose doing shall win me a right to rest. So I followed the servant who summoned me, thinking to go straight to the Cardinal Colonna's presence. But when I came to the chamber through which I must pass to the room where I was used to find him they told me that I must wait. His Eminence was not alone, and must not be disturbed until those who were with him had finished their business.

So I was left to myself, my mind full of the days when Emilia Colonna lived in these very places, when her eyes gazed upon these painted ceilings, and these carven chairs, and these dim

tapestries. Here, perhaps, when her heart was
hot with love, she had waited for the lover who
sat within to-day. Here, perhaps, she had given
back his kisses and his love. Here had that
dishonor been wrought which with every breath
I expiate in my living life. Full of such
thoughts I stood alone.

How long I waited I cannot tell. A hand
was laid upon my shoulder, and aroused me to
myself. I turned about and knew that it was
Filippa, who had glided in unheard. Her face
was full of such wrath as might have flashed
from the faces of the old goddesses of the
pagans. Never had I so seen the full splendor
of her face and her form. She moved toward
me noiselessly, but it was with no petty cunning
that she governed her motion; her stealthy
step had the grandeur of a lion's as she came
close to me, and spoke in low tones fiercer than
loud threats.

She knew why I was come, she said. It was
to tell her kinsfolk tales of where I had found
her. Well, I might speak them out if I would.

She would swear that they were lies, and that I told them because I had insolently dared whisper words of love to her, and she had scorned me.

" Which will be believed? " she asked, — " you, a stranger from God knows where, or I, a Roman lady? Speak if you will."

So she stood for a moment, in all the splendor of her beauty. But that beauty, which when I saw it first filled me with such delight as the Grecian artist felt when at his prayer the marble was turned to flesh, filled me now with loathing. For it seemed the incarnate beauty of this Old World, that for ages has led men on to such nameless fates as that which I suffer. I shrank away from her, with some movement as if I would thrust her aside. What was she to me? I had warned her of what might come. She had scorned my warning. Let her glide on to her fate.

But of a sudden, when she saw that I was not moved, her whole face changed; her lip trembled; her eyes filled with tears. She snatched my hand, and held it fast. In God's

name, she begged me, forgive her for speaking
as in her folly she had spoken. In God's name,
have pity. A word from me might set them on
Luigi's track, might drag him to the prison that
meant a living death. Be silent, she prayed
me, for his sake, not for hers.

"For I love him," she sobbed, "I love him
with all my soul."

I looked on her in wonder. My heart soft-
ened; for I saw that even as her threats were
falsehood, her tears and her love were truth.
I laid my hand upon her dark hair, for she
had bent down before me as she clasped my
hand.

"My poor child," I said, "if you love him,
why do you give yourself to the other?"

She looked up piteously. How could she
help it? she asked. A girl must do as her
kinsfolk bid. But all the kin in all the earth
cannot bind the heart.

Then, before I could answer her, there was a
sound of people coming; and in an instant she
had left me, and vanished like a dream.

In another moment there came from the room where the Cardinal Colonna sat, a company of priests, talking in low tones among themselves of what matters I could not tell. But more than once I heard them speak the name of the Cardinal Giulio Colonna, and the name of the Pope. With them was the Florentine Dei Bardi, his thin visage full of eagerness as he spoke to one with a great golden cross, who seemed the chief of the party. With no look at me, who stood aside, they passed by. And as I looked at them I thought how strangely different was this busy company of churchly statesmen from the boyish singers who in the garb of the same Church had chanted through Rome the praises of the martyred saint; how different, too, from the saint who had given her all for Christ when Christ and His Church were poor.

When these figures had passed, I was free to enter the room of the Cardinal Colonna. So I passed within, and found him alone.

He sat in the great carven chair where I

had seen him in the days of our friendship. He
rested his head on his hand. And it seemed
to me that I had never seen living man look
so old and feeble. When he turned his face
toward me, the eyes, which I had been used to
see full of a life that belied the weakness of
his form, were dull as the yellow skin of his
shrunken face. And they were sunken deep
in their sockets, and dark lines were about
them such as they say are about the eyes of
the dead.

There was no look of welcome in his face.
He moved one hand and bade me sit. Then for
a while he looked at me with a strange sternness, .
passionless yet firm, such as some judge might
have when he spoke at last a sentence, with a
broken heart.

"I have sent for you to-day," he said, "because there is no other way. Since you crossed
my path I have known no rest. I have prayed
for it. I have spoken my secrets in the ear of
the Church; but the sacrament itself has not
brought me peace. The olden time with all its

sins is about me still. It is you who have
brought it back, even in the very chapel where
my bones shall lie. What you are, man or devil,
I cannot tell ; but I have grown to know that
until I speak out to you the secrets that you
have called back into life, they will haunt me
still. So I shall speak them out. Then at last
I may give my mind to those things which alone
must fill it now."

Then he looked with his dull eyes, not at
me nor at anything that was about him. But
the holiness that men were used to see in his
face was gone. As he looked to-day, Magdalene might have looked when her eyes were
not yet raised to Heaven.

I spoke no word; but listened as with slow
accents he forced himself to tell me the tale
of Emilia Colonna. In the old days, he said,
when he was a thoughtless boy, his solemn
brother had brought home the bride whom all
men saw with envy. Then at first he himself
had been full of pride that she bore his name,
and had thought no evil as he grew to think

of her more and more. But at last one day they wandered together in a Roman garden, which from times long past has been the pleasure ground of his race. There they spoke of Italy, — the Italy that Dante dreamed of, the Italy that Macchiavelli of Florence longed for in the far-off days when men saw no hope of its coming. And sitting together on a great stone bench, among the flowers, they looked into one another's eyes, and their lips met, and they knew that they loved. Then while slow-witted Pietro was busy in the service of the Church, the lovers used to meet, and to love, and to talk of their love and of Italy. So they had wandered together among the flowers of the garden where first they had loved; and life to them had been full of sunshine and of beauty, and the world free from misery.

The story was the story which had filled my mind as it had filled his. Each word awoke to living life old memories that even as they lay half dead within me had caused me such agony as I had deemed that man could hardly bear.

But I bade myself remember that if this tale brought peace to him, it was best that I should listen, and bear his burdens along with mine: such suffering, perchance, was part of the duty I was born to do. So at last he came close to the time when Pietro Colonna met his end ; and I began to feel that soon I might go and bear away the load of misery from which Giulio had striven to free his soul. But of a sudden I found that he was telling things that I had not known before.

For he told how the lovers of Italy, to whom he had given all his confidence, found that they were pressed too hard by the watchfulness of Pietro. In secret conclave they doomed him to die. Then Giulio's heart revolted. There was little time ; and even then Emilia waited for him in a spot where they were used to meet. Thither he came ; and when he saw her he clasped her fast in his arms, and pressed his lips to hers once more, for the last time. Then he told her how the end of their joys was come. They must part ; and he must go to his death.

With flashing eyes she started up, swearing that
it was a lie, that he loved her no more ; and chose
a pretext to cast her off. But very solemnly
he answered that the end was come indeed ; and
he charged her to warn Pietro, and begged her
to pray for his wretched self. Then he left her,
sitting with her head flung back, pale as death ;
and her firm-shut lips spoke no word of farewell.
From that he went and made ready for the
death to which his treachery doomed him, for
the friends whom he had betrayed would suffer
no traitor to live. But though he went to his
death, he felt that a load was off his soul. So
he came to his lodging, and there found waiting
for him a note from Emilia. "I love you,
Giulio," she wrote ; "I will not speak. You
and I shall belong to one another in the sight
of men." When he read those lines his heart
stood still. With all his speed he hurried to
the palace of Pietro. There he found that Pietro was already dead ; and Emilia waited above,
to clasp him in her treacherous arms even while
Pietro lay warm in his blood.

" Then at last," he said, " I knew what our
sin had been; and full of horror, I vowed that
all the rest of my life should be one long pen-
ance, which, perchance, might win us the mercy
of God. So I gave myself to God, whom I have
striven to serve from that day forth. May He
have mercy on my soul !"

With that he bowed his head and covered his
face with his hands. And I stood still, full of
such loathing of myself as I had not dreamed
of before. For the sin which I bear upon my
soul I knew at last in all its nakedness. I had
thought it such sin as men do in the weakness
of the flesh. Now I knew that to that sin which
had seemed enough was added such dishonor
as I had not deemed in my living life that men
could work. In my misery I groaned aloud.
And when I groaned, he lifted up his head once
more ; and I saw that his face grew stern.

Leave him, he bade me. Let him never see
my face again. I had tortured him until he
had spoken. In God's name, let me trouble him
no more.

So I turned to go; and he, gathering his strength, sat watching me, as with trembling steps I passed from his presence.

.   .   .   .

There are tales of men, chased like me by the spectres of old crime, who have come after long years to the judges and bidden them speak a sentence. They were happier than I; for human law-givers would laugh at my tale. I would fain raise against myself the hand of justice, and hiding from my eyes before their time the sunshine of the world, seek rest in my grave. But then I think of what I was and of what I am. Who knows into what form the sinful spirit that is mine might go if it were loosed from this? There are tales at which scholars smile, of wicked souls who prowl on the earth in the bodies of foul beasts.

No. What I am I must be, until in the mercy of God the end of what I am shall come. In old Rome Emilia sinned. She sinned with the world about her, — a world that knew not honor or truth. The light of her life was love. She loved with all her earthly heart; and all things were bent before her love. So she did what her love counselled, even to the foulest of dishonor; and to the very end she knew no repentance. Then, in our New England, where the hearts of men are as pure as the clear air they breathe, I was born and was taught the lessons of my people; and I grew to hate falsehood and dishonor, and to hold myself above the herd of sinners. But in quiet hours I was always sad with a sadness of which I could not guess the meaning. Now I know it, as none could know it who was not reared in all the purity of the home that I shall see no more. And I must not shrink; but living on, must ever be with my sin-stained self, until perhaps a time may come when deeds of mine may win the mercy of God.

Yes. The life that is must atone for the sins done in the life that is past. So on this earth must it ever be, until at length to all human life shall come rest like that from which, at the voice of God, it first awakened.

Here, I think, I may add a few lines from another letter of Cleveland's to my father.

"Beverly," he writes, "we hardly see. He cannot forgive Abby for caring about his soul, or me for taking care of my business reputation. After all, you know, we painters have to think about our clients. Beverly glides back and forth on the stairways here, as grim as you please. It is as much as ever that he will bow to me. Such unreasonable conduct in anybody else would make me real mad, as the boys used to say. But of course it would be absurd to treat Beverly as if he were like ordinary human beings. Besides, do you know, I cannot help feeling rather anxious about him. There is a queer look in his eyes. If I had any sort of authority in the matter, I should be inclined to engage somebody to watch him. He needs watching, I fear, as much as his father did. What a hideous thing this insanity is.

"By the way, is there any truth in these rumors about the Franklin Mills? The last dividend was smaller than I expected."

XIV.

From Beverly's Journal.

A S I came down the staircase of the Colonna palace, bound I know not whither, I saw just within the entrance door the black figure of Dei Bardi. He was speaking hurriedly to a servant, whom he held close by the wall so that they could not be seen from without; and he pointed with a hand that shook with excitement toward something from which they were separated by the wall. Then I saw the servant nod his head, as if he understood the charge that was given him; but in spite of Monsignor's excitement the fellow passed out of the door with no hurried step. It seemed, indeed, as if he studied to appear unconcerned. It seemed as if the priest so studied too; for when the man was gone he gathered himself together and stood still for a moment. Then, with his head bent down like one in deep thought, he slowly stepped out of the door too, and turned in the direction in which the servant had not gone. But I saw his eyes peering out from under the broad brim of his hat, to make sure that something before him was really what he deemed it.

So when I passed out of the door in his footsteps I 'looked the same way, curious to know what had so moved him. Before me stood a man of the people, leaning lazily against the palace wall. If I had not seen that Dei Bardi thought him no common sight I should have passed him without a look; but now that my attention was aroused, I looked at him closely, and knew him for the man I had seen in the church of Santa Emilia, — the Count Luigi.

He was come here, perhaps, in the wild hope that he might catch a glimpse of Filippa's face, that he might see a loving look in the eyes that would know him in spite of his mean dress. Not thinking of his danger, he waited, while his enemies were gone on either side to fetch the officers who should seize him. A few moments more, and he would be carried off to the prison whence the foes of the Pope do not emerge.

I could lose no time, and I could not bid him fly, for wherever he went he would meet the enemies that were gathering about him. So, with no thought save for his safety, I called his name in a low voice and beckoned him to come within the palace door. When he heard me call him he looked up; and a great curse sprang to his lips as he saw that I knew him.

"Take care," he said between his teeth, as he came toward me. "You call yourself my friend, and you track me like a dog who follows his master unbidden, and licks his hand when the enemy is upon him. Such dogs are struck down."

I made no answer to his threat, but in hurried words told him his danger. Then, for I thought of no other way to save him, I placed in his hand the key of my rooms, and bade him hurry thither and there hide himself until

such time as he might find to come forth un-
noticed.

As he heard me speak he looked at me with
wonder. Did I know, he asked me, that what
I proposed meant a prison for me too? For he
who shields the enemies of the Pope makes
himself of their number.

I answered him that I cared nothing for that.
Let him hasten, or he would be too late.

"Do you know," he asked, "what I should
say if you were one of my people? I should
say that this was a trap; that you loved Filippa
yourself and would take this way to clear me
from your path. And I would kill you here;
and wait for Dei Bardi if he ever came."

His words made me angry. Do as he would,
I bade him; I could do no more. And I turned
away, ready to pass into the narrow street. But
just as I turned he seized my hand, and drew
me back.

"I will trust you," he said; "you have been
reared in a land of freedom and of truth."

With that he left me, and glided swiftly up

the great stairway. And I went out into the
street. For in Rome I have learned to dis-
semble; I have breathed in the lesson with
the Roman air; perhaps there has risen to life
within me some memory of the old wiles that
Emilia Colonna cast about her. And even
though what Luigi said was true, and I had
indeed been reared in a land where frankness
and truth are the habit of men, the thought
that rose uppermost in my mind was that I
must act as if I had not known that Luigi was
by, lest Monsignor, who perhaps had seen me
on the stairway behind him, might be roused
to wonder why I had turned back.

So forth I went into the Roman sunshine.
And as I passed the corner of a street close by,
I saw the black-robed priest, no longer deep
in pretended thought, hurrying toward me with
officers at so swift a pace that his black cloak
swelled behind him in the wind. When he
came in sight of the palace and saw that Luigi
was no longer there, I heard him utter a great
oath of anger. Then he quickened his pace,

beckoning the officers to follow. And I went another way, and wandered for a while about the Roman streets.

Then by and by, when I thought that time enough had passed for no one to look askance at me, I came back and passed up the stone stairway. There nothing met me save the shadows of the olden time that fall upon my soul when I pass the spot where the olden time worked out its doom. So I came to my own door, where I knocked gently; and the Count Luigi opened it.

When he saw me his face was lighted with a look of welcome greeting. He drew me within the door; and when the door was closed behind me, he flung his arms about me as he had flung them when we met on the stairway, on the day when Filippa pledged her faith to Palchi. He pressed me close to his heart, pouring forth a flood of grateful words. He had wronged me. He had let himself believe that I would betray him, that I did not hold him dear. And now I had proven that I was the faithful friend he had been used to deem me ; I had saved his life from his enemies. He would roll at my feet, craving pardon for the thought that had wronged me. He would tear out the part of his heart that had swerved from trust in me. So he spoke, with all the passion of his people.

When the first tempest of his speech was over, I asked him why he was come back to Rome, where every door-way might be a trap.

He thrust his hand into his breast and drew forth a dagger.

"I will tell you," he said. " It was to drive this into Palchi's heart. He shall not live to call Filippa his wife."

I looked at him startled. I had not dreamed that the passion of his love had swept him on so far. And he, with growing anger, told me how the time was running short, how in few days the hour would come when Palchi should claim his bride. He had tried to bear the thought that this hour was at hand, to trust fate that in future time he might come to his love and laugh with her in secret at her dapper husband; but when he thought how Palchi was to call her his, to clasp her, even loveless, in his thin arms, all Luigi's heart rose up in protest. He swore an oath that Palchi should die. Before Heaven, he swore to me again, he would keep his oath. I had saved him that he might keep it. To-day he had known that Palchi was to pass within the Colonna palace, on some errand with the Cardinal Giulio. At the palace door he had stood waiting; and when the prince stepped forth it would have been to meet an unshriven death. Unkind fate had thrown Dei Bardi in his way; then Heaven had sent me to save him, that Palchi might die. For die he should; there was still time.

I shrank from him, filled as he was with sinful thoughts. What good, I asked him, could come of such a deed? More than ever it would part him from Filippa.

" Yes," he said, " they will put me to death. But I shall sleep quiet in my grave; for the man that has stolen my love will be as cold as I."

Let him beware, I cried, full of the agony that lay hidden in the grave of Emilia. Those who die in sin may not sleep in peaceful graves.

Then he laughed aloud. I was always prating of sin, he said. Life was sin to me. Love was sin. Then, as he spoke, his cheek began to burn and his eye to flash with fresh fire.

Did I know, he asked me, what my prating of sin had led to? It had led to this; and he held up the dagger again before my eyes.

What he meant I could not tell. I bade him speak plain.

In Emilia's church, he told me, he had come to meet Filippa, who had slipped away in secret from her people. Thence he had planned that they should fly together to the secret places where his friends lay hidden. There, with hearts full of love for one another and for Italy, they would have laughed when they thought of the baffled folk in Rome : of grim Dei Bardi, biting his. nails in vexation; of the stern Countess, filling her palace with impotent curses ; of trim Palchi, strutting and showing his teeth, the laughing-stock of the town ; of pious Cardinal Giulio, praying that all men might be saved. Then I had come between them, and unknowing had checked their flight. Now it was too late. He could not make his plans again. There was nothing left but this : again he held the knife in his hand.

I looked at him, sick at heart. I made no answer. Was this, I thought, my mission in the wretched life that I may not cut short? Must I spread about me, in the form that is mine, evil and misery and guilt, even as in the olden time Emilia Colonna spread them about her path? Longing to do good, to win my right to the salvation that I have dared to hope for in the time that is to come, must I unwittingly spurn from me and cast down into sin deep as that from which I struggle to be free, the souls of the men that are about me? It were better, I thought, that I should rest among the damned.

What look was in my face I know not ; but it must have been a strange one. For as the Count Luigi gazed upon me I saw him grow pale. He seized my arm. In Heaven's name, he asked me, what was in my mind?

I shook my head. I could not speak. I was full of that nameless agony which falls upon me at those times of my life when a little more of what is to come is revealed to me at last. The writhing clouds that make past and present seem like one long evil dream from which there is no waking were gathered before my eyes. It seemed to me that the walls which were about me, that the startled man who stood before me, were made of such vapors as curl thick through summer skies. A breath of wind might change their quivering forms to a shapeless mist, dark and murky and fearful.

Then I heard the Count Luigi cry out again in passion. Was I faithless after all? Would I betray him because I was pleased to say that what he did was sinful? By Heaven, I should be the first to feel the sin!

What happened then I know not; for the winds of confusion broke in upon the vapors that writhed about me, and all was darkness, in which I struggled I knew not whither. But when at last the light gleamed upon me once more, and I knew myself, and where I was and what I did, I was standing erect on the spot where I had stood before. And in my hand was the dagger which the Count Luigi had held; and the Count Luigi, pale and trembling, lay at my feet, as if he had been flung down; and I was speaking and he listening, as if my words were the words of a prophet.

Then I stretched out my hand and raised him, and I bade him be of good cheer and trust me, for all should be well with him.

For the writhing clouds were gone, and I saw the light of God's day; and by it I knew that though the deeds by which I may win my right to rest were still afar off, there was a deed that I might do even now which should save from sin these friends who suffered before my eyes the first agonies of lives that without me might end in agony like mine.

Be of good cheer, I bade him again. Trust in me; and I would make Filippa his before the eyes of God and men; and Palchi should live, to strut in Rome until he found another bride to dower with his millions; and on Filippa's soul and Luigi's there should be no stain of sin to darken the love that should fill their lives until Heaven called them to the rest of its eternities.

Then the Count Luigi slowly rose up, and with trembling voice told me that he knew not my meaning, but that he could not help trusting one that spoke as I spoke, for my words were no words of earth. And bending down, he kissed my hand.

With that I bade him go hide himself in an inner chamber until I should call him forth; and thither he went. Then, left alone, I gathered up my strength and prepared to do the work that should save him, praying in my heart that in good time the light might come which should show to me the work that shall win the salvation which is rest for the soul that I call mine.

XV.

BEFORE I set out I looked within the room where Luigi was gone, on whose service I was bound. Tired out, he had fallen asleep, and slept peacefully as a child. So might Giulio have slept in the olden time, when his life was still free from sin, smiling as he dreamed of the woman, the thought of whom was joy. I looked at Luigi, keeping very still for fear that I might arouse him. I found myself unawares speaking words of blessing, such as old folk speak. For though I seem near to Luigi in years, my soul-life runs back in the past; and with it runs memory, until I feel older than any gray-beard. Then I left him gently resting, and made my way to Giulio Colonna's door.

They would have kept me out, but˙I gave them gold, whereat they grinned and bowed as they might have bowed before an angel. So I passed in, and coming to the room where Giulio Colonna sits, I entered as I had been used to enter in the days of our friendship, unannounced.

The Cardinal Giulio sat alone as I had seen him sit before ; but his look was different from any that I had known as his. Deep in thought I had seen him ; full of concern and trouble, too ; at other times calm and smiling ; but never until now full of busy life. His back was turned to me, as he sat in his carven chair, leaning forward over his table. I could hear the sharp scratching of his pen, for he was writing swiftly, like the bustling merchants whom I used to watch at home in their dreary counting-houses. In his bearing there was no trace of age or of reverence. Of old he had been a man apart from the world ; now he seemed of the world, straining every nerve in the race of life.

When he heard my step, he did not turn his head or stop his writing ; but raising his left hand with a gesture of beckoning, he spoke in a low voice words which I could not hear. I stepped closer to him. In a moment he spoke again, with some shade of displeasure in his tone.

"I have asked you, Monsignor," he said, ".what news you bring of Capellari."

For a little while I did not perceive his meaning, so full was my mind of what I was come to say to him ; so I made no answer. Then of a sudden I remembered how there were stories abroad in Rome that Pope Gregory was ailing, and that churchmen were busying their brains about who should be his successor. Of these tales I had thought little, for to me it mattered not who sat in the Vatican. But here before me was one to whom it mattered much ; and full of the thought of what might come to him he asked me, whom he thought his wily chaplain, for news of the man whose death he longed for. I was sick at heart, thinking how far his mind had travelled from such thoughts as I had hoped to find it busy with. And he, when I did not speak, stopped his pen and turned about, his face full of displeasure.

"Do you not hear my question?" he began. Then, when he saw who was with him, he flung down his pen and sat erect facing me, his features flushed with anger.

By what right, he asked me, was I come thither? He had bidden me come no more. He had spoken out those things which the spells I cast upon him had forced from his lips. As he spoke he grew troubled. My presence seemed to bring back the old thoughts that he had put aside. In God's name, he cried, leave him in peace! Go, or he would have me thrust forth by his lackeys.

Then I spoke to him gently. It was for no affair of mine nor of his, I said, that I was come. For my sake and for his I would have left him in peace with all my heart, and borne with no groans those burdens of his which he had laid upon me, even as I bore my own. It was for the sake of others that I was come, of others

whom he loved; and, with the blessing of
Heaven, I would come before him no more on
this earth if he would let me speak to-day.

He looked at me for a moment without an
answer, his face full of anger and of doubt.
Nay, it seemed that in his eye there was some
touch of fear. For though he could not know
what I am, he could not but feel that I am
such a thing as never crossed his path before.
Old sins in this earth lie buried to rise only
when the day of reckoning shall come; but I,
by that strange doom that is half a blessing,
walk the earth, a living sin. I cast my shadow
upon all about me; and most of all upon him
who knew me in the form that of old was mine.

Speak, he said at length, but let my words
be numbered, and let them be the last that he
should ever hear from my lips.

So I spoke, with a flood of passion that was
strange to me. My words came to my lips and
I spoke them out unthinking, my heart full of
the mission on which I was come. And Giulio
Colonna listened and was moved. At first

he seemed impatient, longing that I should be done; but as I spoke I saw his face grow grave and passionate, and his eyes flash with a fire as if of sympathy. Then the strength that his form had shown seemed to leave him; and he leaned back in his carven chair, busy with no thoughts save those which I poured forth.

At first, I think, I began to speak of the olden time of which he had told me the story, reminding him how he knew what love might make men do. Blessed by Heaven, no holier power than love dwells on the earth; unblessed, there is no fouler fiend. And that, I told him, none could know better than he, who has prayed through long years to be freed from its curses; nor yet than Emilia, who groans out such agonies as death alone can bring.

When I spoke her name he moaned aloud, but I did not check my speech; and presently he asked me why I dragged his sins back from the grave.

Then I told him that it was to show into what dangers others might fall. And he asked me what others I meant, and what they had to do with him. And I told him that I meant the girl whom he was giving over to a loveless wedlock. Thereupon he asked me what I knew of her. And I said that by chance I knew more than he.

With that he turned upon me with a face of such passion as in all my life I had never seen. Had I dared, he cried, to play the knave within his doors? Then, by Heaven, I should feel what he could do!

But when he spoke thus I broke into anger too, and cried out louder than he. Was his mind so foul, I asked him, that even in the quiet of the home that he had made holy with his prayers, he could harbor no thought of purity? Then truly the curse that had fallen upon him when he sinned with Emilia was upon him still in all its blackness. And I spoke more to the same end, full of anger; and presently I saw that he was struck with shame. For he bent down his head, and spoke gently, bidding me tell him what, then, my words had meant.

A simple thing, I answered him. Only that

Filippa, whom he would sell to grinning Palchi, loved another as dearly as in the olden time Emilia had loved him. By a strange chance the knowledge of this love was come to me; and now I brought it to him, so that he might draw back in time, and check the fresh beginning of work such as had wrought the misery of his life. For in loving wedlock the girl might still live pure, and give to the world children on whom she could look without a blush, in the pride of holy motherhood. But if she should wed as he' bade her, then in the ages to come he should hear her groans mingled with the groans of Emilia rising above the echoes of hell. And even though he who heard might be sitting among the blessed, he should sit there damned by the knowledge that deeds of his had set these sinners a-groaning.

So I called upon him, in the name of the dead Emilia, to stop this work before it was too late ; to cast off Palchi, to join Filippa to her love. I called upon him in the name of Emilia, in mine own.

In God's name, he asked me, who was I that spoke?

Then I found that I could not tell him, for something bade me keep back the truth. But this I said: I was one who had sinned as in the olden time Emilia had sinned; who knew tortures like hers; who would give my life-blood to save another from such a life as I dragged out in agony deeper than the agony which he had known through all the years of his repentance. For my sake, I cried again, for the sake of one who knows as no other living thing can know what comes to those who have forgotten the commands of God, let no such work begin again!

Then I saw that he was greatly moved; for his face was very pale and very grave. And it seemed as if in the depths of his heart there was such a struggle as heaven wages with hell when the souls of men are at stake. And presently he asked me who the man was whose cause I came to plead. And I told him that it was the Count Luigi.

When he heard that name his anger blazed up afresh. Did I know, he asked me, of whom I spoke? He had cherished the Count Luigi as he would have cherished his own child ; and with black treachery Luigi had turned upon him and betrayed him to his enemies. Yes ; and the treachery with which I charged Luigi in stealing Filippa's heart made the old treachery doubly black. This creature whose cause I came to plead had done his best to overthrow the structure which he, — Giulio Colonna, — this creature's greatest benefactor, had reared with the labor of all his lifetime. And to serve the pleasure of this traitor I would have him break his pledged word. The plan was mad. So he raved on in his anger.

When he paused I spoke very solemnly. Did I guess his meaning aright? I asked him. Had he set his heart, as men said that he had set it, on Saint Peter's chair? And had the Count's flight made men whisper that the Count's friends were privy to the plots of those who work against the Pope? Beneath the holy

14

surface of his daily life, was his heart in truth full of such wiles as his grinning chaplain, with all his art, had not the art to conceal ? Did he, — Giulio, with his white hair and his saint's face, — still pant for the prizes of this world ?

What right had I, he cried, to catechise him ?

The right, I told him, of one who was come to warn him in time. Let him with all his heart fall to the prayers that in the past he had only mouthed. Let him, as he hoped for pardon and salvation in the world to come, — and soon to come for him, — cast aside all care for what might chance in this.

In God's name, he cried, had not his fastings and his prayers won him freedom from thoughts like these ?

Then I told him that freedom from thoughts like these comes only when God's judges have spoken words of mercy to a pardoned soul. As he hoped for that mercy, let his only thoughts on earth be of what good he might still do to make amends for the evil that in the past he had wrought. Unknowing, I was come with a message of salvation to him too, who stood in sorer need even than those whom I would check from plunging into sin. As he loved his soul, let not that message pass unheeded!

How could he know, he cried, that what I said was not all a lie?

Send for Filippa, I told him. Ask her for the truth.

Even as I spoke the door opened, and Dei Bardi stood before us. Some message of state-craft was on his lips, for before he saw me he had spoken the name of Capellari. But when he saw that the Cardinal Giulio was not alone, he stood still, his broad-brimmed hat in his hand, his face full of stern business.

"I must speak with His Eminence," he said almost roughly.

With no answer, I turned to Giulio Colonna and bade him send the priest for Filippa. He looked upon me full of surprise, for in all the years that had passed since he had been a prince of the Church no man had dared speak to him as I spoke. I did not hesitate. I spoke to him again, bidding him, as he loved his soul, send the priest to fetch the girl.

Then, very slowly, the Cardinal Giulio turned to Dei Bardi, and told him that he could hear no message, for he had business with Filippa, whom he prayed that the priest would summon. And in the depths of my heart I thanked God that I had won my fight.

The black-robed priest, seized with astonishment, spoke some word of remonstrance, whereat Giulio's wrath was aroused once more. With a burst of passion as fierce as the Count Luigi's, he bade the priest hasten to do what he had commanded. No man should disobey his word.

" Go ! " he cried. And Dei Bardi, with a low bow, glided off, amazed. Before long he came back, saying that the girl was at hand. Then Giulio, who had said no word since the priest had left us, bade him wait without until he was summoned. So, full of vexation, he withdrew; and presently Filippa came.

When she saw that I was there, her face blazed with such anger as in the faces of

Grecian gods struck death to the hearts of men. Was I come after all, she cried, to persecute her with my lies?

Very gently I answered her that she had best go ask the Cardinal Colonna what I had said; and as she loved her happiness and her soul she had best speak the truth.

Very gently, then, the Cardinal Giulio beckoned her to come to him, and took her by the hand, and spoke to her in a whisper that I could not hear. And I, turning aside, saw that I was close to the crucifix where the Cardinal Giulio was used to pray in the hours of his trouble. So I kneeled me down, and prayed in silence that the work which I was about might prosper; that these lives which my life had crossed might be blessed by my passage; that Giulio and Luigi and Filippa might be saved from such misery as mine; and that, when God in Heaven deemed that my hour was come, some light might gleam to me over the path by which I might struggle on to the salvation which is rest.

Then, when my prayer was done, and once more I began to listen to what was going on about me, I heard the sound of weeping. And turning about, I saw Filippa kneeling at Giulio's feet, her face hidden in his robes, her form quivering with great sobs; and Giulio's old eyes were full of tears, and his thin hand with its gleaming jewel stroked her black hair, and his face was as gentle as the face of an angel. Then I knew that he was saved, and that she was saved, and that the words he whispered in her ear were the words that bore from God the message of their salvation. So, full of gratitude that my prayer for them had been answered, I knelt again, and poured forth a flood of thanksgiving, trusting that in days to come the mercy that has been shown to them may at last be shown to me.

XVI.

WITH these words Beverly's journal ends.
The manuscript breaks off abruptly in
the middle of a page. There is no record of
how or when the last lines were written; but
from what I have been able to learn of the rest of
his story I have grown to think that there was
but one time when he could have written them.
This was during the last hours of the day when
he had found Luigi at the palace door and had
gone from him to the Cardinal Colonna. There
is nothing except what happened afterwards to
show how his interview with the Cardinal and
Filippa ended. From what happened afterwards, however, I feel sure that it was short.
Beverly must have told them where Luigi lay
hidden; the Cardinal must have promised that
in the quiet of the night he would bring the girl
up the palace stairs to the chamber where her

lover waited, and there join them with the blessing of the Church. Then they should go in peace to some place of safety.

I like to think, then, that in the early hours of the night, while Beverly and Luigi watched together for those who were coming, Beverly took his pen, and wrote in his book the thoughts that troubled his brain. I like to think, too, that in writing them he found such comfort as men always find in speaking out, even to deaf leaves of paper. It is your silent men, who keep all things to themselves, that go mad. Richard Beverly's father, they say, had no friends to whom he opened his heart, and, like many another prudent man, held that one who wrote down what might not be read by all the world was a fool. By and by he cut his throat. Richard Beverly's mother left reams of sentimental journals behind her, and lived to a good old age.

So I like to think of Richard Beverly, in his great chamber lighted by a single candle, turning to these pages that received his secrets forty years ago, and writing them down while Rome slept about him, in the last days of the old papal rule. I like to think that as he wrote he sighed with the relief of one who for a time at least lays aside his burden. I like to think that all the while the gallant young Roman, whose happiness Beverly had wrought that day, waited beside him in the dim light, with throbbing heart, and ears strained to catch the sound of the footsteps that should tell him of his coming bride. I like to think that the sound of those footsteps came as the last lines in the old journal were writing; that Richard Beverly flung down his pen where he was, and went and opened his door, and that there he found the old Cardinal and Filippa. I like to think that when this faded ink was still wet, the Count Luigi was clasping his love in his arms, while Richard Beverly and the Cardinal Giulio Colonna stood aside with brimming eyes, as they thought of the unblessed loves of Emilia that in a happier time might have been as pure as these. But this is all a fancy.

What comes afterwards I have learned partly from letters of Cleveland's, partly from traditions of what Cleveland wrote and said about the last hours of Beverly's life. For Cleveland died years ago, and so did his wife, — long before I was old enough to know anything about these matters, which nobody else could have told me. So I have had to put the tale together as best I could ; but in so doing I have come to feel as if every word that I wrote were true.

What I shall write next happens to be pretty well authenticated. To be sure, the letter in which Cleveland wrote it down has been lost ; but I have talked with people who read it for themselves, and I find that all the versions agree in the main.

In the middle of the night, — the same night, it must have been, when Beverly wrote the last words in his journal, — there came a low knock at Cleveland's door. Whereupon Cleveland, who was a light sleeper, rose, with sundry oaths that he should be disturbed at such an hour, and went to see who disturbed him. To his surprise he found Beverly, who had not deigned to visit him for some weeks. And Beverly, without waiting for any formalities, told the artist that he must put on his clothes and come with him, on a matter of life and death.

"There is not a moment to lose," said Beverly. "We must have a man that we can trust; and I know that we can trust you, for you are a gentleman," — a charge, as Cleveland remarked in his letter, to which it was his habit invariably to plead guilty.

So, wondering what on earth was up, Cleveland hurried into his clothes, and climbed the stairs that led to Beverly's rooms.

There they found three figures waiting for them, all wrapped in cloaks. By the light of the single candle that burned in the great room Cleveland could not at first make out their faces; but presently he was astonished to recognize, in a man who stood as erect as if he had been young, the Cardinal Colonna. For the Cardinal beckoned him forward; and in a few words thanked him for his presence, and told.

him that he had been sent for to witness a marriage which circumstances compelled them to solemnize in secret. Then, without more ado, the Cardinal Colonna turned to the other figures who were with him; and they knelt down, and with a short formal service the Cardinal made them man and wife. Meanwhile Cleveland and Beverly stood by; and Cleveland told how in the candle-light it had seemed to him that the gleam in Beverly's wide-open eyes was the gleam of tears.

When the service was over, the wedded couple kissed the Cardinal's hand. Then they slowly rose, and clasping each other in their arms stood in close embrace, gazing into each other's eyes. Meanwhile the Cardinal Colonna moved toward the table where the candle stood, and bending down signed his name with a firm hand to a paper that lay there. Then he beckoned to Cleveland and to Beverly; and with his thin white finger pointed out the places where they should sign. And when their names were written he took up the paper, and folding it turned to the lovers whom he had joined together, and held it out to them.

"God be with you, my children," he said. "I seal the beginning of your earthly hopes with the end of mine. But my heart is light; for I have done God's will. May He smile on you through all your lives as He smiles on me to-night."

He spoke in a low, firm voice; and the hand that held the paper did not tremble. The lovers turned toward him to take the paper; and, as they turned, Cleveland knew them for the Count Luigi and the Contessina Filippa. The Count took the paper with a look of loving gratitude that meant more, Cleveland wrote, than a whole oration, with applause into the bargain. For all that, the Count was not satisfied with looks, but began to speak his gratitude in words. Whereupon the Cardinal Colonna raised his hand with a gesture of remonstrance, and pointing to Beverly, who stood aside, bade them thank him, to whom all the gratitude was due. Then, before the Count had time to speak again, the Cardinal Colonna himself spoke to Beverly.

" Friend," he said, " I too owe you grateful thanks; for the voice of God tells me in my heart that it is to you that I shall owe my salvation, and to no deeds of mine."

And what the devil it all meant, Cleveland wrote, he could not imagine.

The scene of gratitude was short, however; for Beverly, who seemed more master of himself than any of the others, warned them that there was no time to spare, and blowing out the light, led the way with soft steps to the door-way. Then the whole company slowly and silently passed down the chilly stairway, until they came to the Cardinal Colonna's door. There they left him, the lovers kissing his hand once more, and he once more whispering a word of blessing. And as they crept on down the stairway, they heard his door softly close behind him.

Beverly and Cleveland were side by side in the darkness; the lovers just before them. As they passed on, Cleveland felt his kinsman clutch his arm.

" Cleveland," he heard him whisper, in a tone of strange joy, " the shadows are here no more. What does it mean ? The end is not come, yet the shadows are here no more."

Before Cleveland could answer this speech, which seemed to him a burst of madness, the little company came to the outer door of the palace. There a small gate in the great door stood open. And the lovers, turning once to press Beverly's hand, passed without into the dark street, alone together at last. And whither they went, and what befell them from that time on, I have never known.

Then with stealthy movements Beverly closed the little gate and drew the bolts to. And then, muttering a word of thanks to Cleveland for coming at his bidding, he turned ; and together they set about climbing the stairs once more.

Of a sudden, just as they were close to the Cardinal Colonna's door, a great noise burst upon the quiet of the night. The Cardinal's door was flung open. There was a sound of voices and of hurrying steps within. There was a flash of lights ; and forth rushed a man, shouting in anger,-who turned toward the stair-way where Cleveland and Beverly stood. Who it was Cleveland could not see. Beverly's eyes seemed better.

" It is that black devil!" he cried. " He shall not chase them!" And leaping forward he bade him stop.

The man tried to push him aside ; whereupon Beverly clutched him by the throat. For an instant they struggled on the landing. Then together they pitched headlong down the stone stairs into the darkness below.

In a moment more, there came out of the Cardinal's rooms servants with lights. With them Cleveland hurried down the stairs to the bottom, where all was still. There, side by side, they found the forms of Beverly and Dei Bardi. The priest was dead. His neck was broken. He lay staring upwards, his thin lips parted, his thin cheeks puckered with a grin of agony. He looked, Cleveland wrote, like one who was already in hell.

Beverly lay as quiet as he; but on his face was a look of peace. And as they bent over him they saw that he still breathed; so they lifted him up and gently bore him to Cleveland's chambers. There they laid him on a bed, where he rested with closed eyes.

Meanwhile others bore the priest back to the room whence he had rushed forth. And the Cardinal Giulio Colonna, they say, when they told him what had happened, and that Beverly still lived, said no word; but knelt beside the form of his dead servant, and prayed throughout the Roman night for the wily soul that had given all its wiles to his service.

15

XVII.

O F what happened hereafter among the Romans whose lives Beverly had changed I have no record. Indeed, I care to know nothing of what the Prince Palchi said and did, or of what oaths the angry Countess swore, or of what busied the brains of those churchmen who had plotted with the dead Florentine to place the Cardinal Giulio Colonna on Pope Gregory's seat. For what I am writing is the story of Richard Beverly's life and nothing else. And now I am come close to the end of it.

Born in the clear air of our New England, reared in the simple traditions of a time that still remembered the lessons of the fathers, he was come in his manhood to a world where all was different, — where the air was full of golden haze, where all external life was beautiful and soft, where life stretched back to farthest time,

and with it the roots of the sin that flourished
even in the shadow of God's church. There he
had lived as best he could, never failing the
traditions in which he had been reared. There
his New-World purity had fought and won its
little battle; and had sown in the soil of the
beautiful, corrupt old Rome that Victor Em-
manuel's soldiers have swept from the earth, a
seed of truth and of goodness that I love to
think may still be growing and strengthening
in the new Italy, whose banners now wave in
the Roman sunshine. It was the musket-shot
of Concord that awoke old Europe to liberty.
I like to think that it shall be the mission of
our New World to win her back to purity. But
when I fall to talking as I find that I am writing
now, my sensible friends smile in a pitying way.
Perhaps the whole notion is a wild one, caught
from the madness of poor Richard Beverly with
which I have lived so much of late. I must
back to him, once for all.

After the night when they bore him up the
great stairway and laid him on the bed in

Cleveland's chambers, he lay for days in a stupor. Cleveland was all kindness; and so was his wife, who nursed the sick man as tenderly as a mother. But for days he knew nothing of what was about him; and the doctors who came shook their heads, and said that he might die without awakening to consciousness. Most of the time he rested quietly; but now and then he would utter incoherent words, always in the language of Italy. Finally, as a night more troubled than most was drawing to a close, he began to rave aloud, crying out as if his mind were in a great agony. But by and by his eyes opened wide, with a look of wondering joy, and he lay very still, gazing at something which those about him could not see. His heart seemed too full to speak. The look of joy brightened more and more, till at last he swooned, as one swoons in a summer air too full of the scent of flowers. Then they thought he was dying; but he fell into a short sleep, and finally he opened his eyes and spoke in a low voice, as if he knew at last what words he spoke.

They hurried to his side. There he called them by name, and thanked them for the gentleness with which they had cared for him. But when they asked him what he would have them do, his answer made them think that his mind still wandered ; for he asked them to call Giulio.

Whom did he mean ? they asked.

Then he smiled as if he saw his own folly, and asked them to go and pray that the Cardinal Colonna would come to him. They thought that he was still wandering, that he did not know what he said. But though they spoke gentle words of remonstrance, and tried to soothe him, he would not give up his purpose. Gently smiling, with no touch of anger in his persistence, he kept on asking them to summon the Cardinal Colonna to his side. The Cardinal would come, he said, when they told him that a dying man had words to speak to him, and to him alone, before he could die.

So at last, fearing all the while that the Cardinal Colonna might take great offence at what

they did, they went to him with Beverly's message, encouraging themselves with the thought
that each day a servant of the Cardinal's had
knocked at Cleveland's door to hear news of
the sick man. When they came to the Cardinal's rooms they were not permitted to enter his
presence; but their message was carried to him,
and in return he sent them a word of thanks.
In a few moments he would come, as the sick
man prayed. And hardly had they brought
back this word, when he followed in their footsteps to the room where Beverly lay.

When he stood before them, they say, the
old man seemed as near his end as did the sick
man who lay on his death-bed. For his thin
face was as pale as death; and his steps were
so feeble that it seemed as if he must fall, even
though a servant held his arm on cither side.
But in his face there was a look of such holiness as even those who had known his face
when all Rome said that it was the face of an
angel, had never dreamed of. For if of old his
face had been like that of one who from afar off

looked upon the peace of heaven, now it was like the face of one who dwelt therein. So, with peaceful face and tottering steps, the old Cardinal made his way to Beverly's side, and stood above the sick man.

What passed then passed between those two. The others who were by stood aside, and listened with awe to words which they could not understand. So they kept silent; and the old Cardinal and the sick man were face to face, and seemed not to know that any other men were by.

At first Beverly smiled, and held out his right hand with a feeble movement, as if he had hardly the power to stir it, and all his power came from his will and not from the muscles that had moved his arm in the days of his strength. And the old Cardinal took the wasted hand and held it in his. Then they heard Beverly call him by his name Giulio, in a tone that was full of love.

The Cardinal Colonna started, and gazed down on the sick man with a look of wonder. And Beverly called him by his name again, and told him with a smile that he had known that he would come to hear his message.

Then, with slow words, the old Cardinal prayed the sick man, in the name of God, to tell him who and what he was.

And Beverly answered that he might speak out at last: that the spirit which was passing was the spirit which in the olden time Giulio had loved.

Thereupon, with a loud cry, the Cardinal Colonna uttered the name of Emilia, and bending down over the sick man, looked into his eyes with a look of fear. But Beverly looked up with a loving smile; and the old Cardinal raised himself up full of wonder, and made the sign of the cross, and motioned those who had pressed near him to stand away. So they moved back; and the Cardinal Giulio Colonna stood alone beside the sick man's bed, gazing into his great eyes and listening to the words which he spoke.

Then Beverly told him how he had just awakened from a vision.

"It seemed to me," he said, "that I was in the garden where in the olden time we loved. And whether I was that which I am or that which I was I could not tell. But full of trouble for the sin I had done I knelt among the flowers; and gazing up to the heavens I prayed with all my heart for light, that I might see the way to work out my salvation. It was in the night-time; and as I prayed I found my eyes fixed upon a star that burned brighter than the rest. Then presently its light grew, and spread about me until I could see no other thing, but knelt surrounded by the glory it shed about me. Then I looked into the depths of the glory of the star, and afar off I saw the throne of heaven. And as I looked, there came before the throne one who wore a crown and bore in her hand a palm. Her I knew for the virgin Emilia, who gave her life for Christ in old Rome. Then kneeling before the throne she spoke pitiful words, and prayed that the peace of God might be granted to the soul of one who in the earth had borne her name. And she told how in time past when that soul had hovered above the brink of hell she had prayed for a respite, and the respite had been granted. And now she prayed that the misery it had suffered and the work it had done might be deemed enough. This she prayed in the name of her Lord Christ. Then from out the glory of the throne came a voice that answered her and said, Yet a little while and her prayer should be granted. Then I stretched out my hands and strove to rise into the glory of the star; but I could not. And presently I was kneeling again in the Roman garden, and the star was again only the brightest of the stars that shone in the Roman night. But my heart was troubled no more; for I had heard the promise of peace."

Then his voice stopped, and through his form there went a shiver, and his eyes closed; and those who were about him knew that his spirit was passing, and fell upon their knees. But the

Cardinal Giulio Colonna stood erect, with a face full of such joy as the saints feel when first they enter into their rest. In his right hand he held on high the crucifix, where the eyes of the sick man should see it if by chance they opened once more. And he spoke aloud, in tones of triumph, prayers for a passing soul such as he might speak for one of his own believers. Then by and by the face of Beverly was lighted again with a radiance of joy such as might have shone from it in his vision, when in the star-lit garden the glory of Heaven beamed upon him. Once more his eyes were opened. Once more he spoke.

"Giulio!" he said, "give thanks to God; for the end is come. And the end is peace."

Then he looked with one last look on the crucifix, and closed his eyes; and gently as a little child falls into sleep he ceased to breathe.

Then the Cardinal Giulio Colonna, first looking down to be assured that Beverly was no more, turned his face heavenward, and in a loud

voice spoke the words of praise that the saints
have taught to the lips of men : —

" *Gloria Patri et Filio et Spiritui Sancto :
sicut erat in principio et nunc et semper in saecula
saeculorum.*"

CONCLUSION.

HERE, I' thought, the story of Richard Beverly should have ended; and when I wrote the last words I put it aside feeling that my work was done. But afterwards I happened to go back to Rome, where more than ever the traces of the old papal times are being swept away. I saw new fragments of the Forum; and new boulevards; and dashing young officers, in jackets trimmed with Astrachan fur; and Piedmontese soldiers, with floating plumes of dark feathers, marching to the sound of the bugle; and amid all the bustle of modern life, staring King Humbert himself, driving with his fairfaced queen, while thin Pope Leo sulked in his prison of the Vatican.

More than ever I felt that the Rome of which I had written, — the Rome where Richard Beverly came to meet his end, — was a shadowy thing that had vanished from the earth. I rubbed my eyes, wondering if after all it had been anything but a dream. Nor, indeed, did I feel that it was much more real when I went without the gate of Saint Paul, and there, in the burying-place where Keats and Shelley lie in the shadow of the monument that the gold of the Roman Cestius built for him in the days of the Emperors, found among the flowers a little stone on which was cut the name of Beverly.

But by and by I made my way again to the church of Santa Emilia. There the same old *custode* I had seen before unlocked the gates of the Colonna chapel, and followed me within them to tell in his cracked old voice how like Paradise its marble glories were. Like Paradise indeed they were in one respect; for they were in no way changed. They were just as they had been in the days when the popes still ruled Rome, when Beverly found here the key to his life-mystery. Here, just as they had been, were the blazing marbles that the old princes had brought together to gladden their burial-place.

Here was the tomb of Emilia Colonna just as Beverly had seen it.

At least, so I thought until I fell to talking with the old *custode*, to whom I would not listen when I came to the chapel before. This time I was less surly; and perhaps with time the old man had grown even more garrulous. For I found myself, after a while, listening with interest to his tales of the Colonnas, and to his laments that the race was no more.

Were they all dead? I asked him.

All, he said, with a sigh and a shake of the head. Then, tottering over to a corner of the chapel, he stood above a simple slab in the floor, which I had not noticed; and pointing to it with his bony hand, he croaked out that here lay the last, who had been laid there forty years ago.

I looked at the slab. There were but three words carved thereon:—

IVLIVS · COLVMNA · CARDINAL

He would have it just so, the old *custode* told me. He was a very holy man, full of humility,

— very holy indeed. They used to say that if he had not died before Pius the Ninth was made pope he might have been made pope himself. But the old *custode* did not believe this story; the Cardinal Colonna had doubtless been a very holy man, but — And here the old fellow shook his wrinkled head, and slowly tapped his forehead with his gnarled finger.

What did he mean? I asked. Did the Cardinal's mind fail?

Well, that was as one might please to think. For his part, the old *custode* did not see how a man whose mind was clear could choose to lie under a miserable little slab when he might have had a tomb fit to take with him to Paradise. Besides, just before he died, the old Cardinal had had a strange fancy. He had insisted that they should add to the epitaph of one of his kinsfolk who lay here some words that meant nothing, and that quite destroyed the effect of the sculpture. A man whose mind was clear would have known better than to deface such carving as this to make room for words that had no meaning.

The old *custode* had hobbled across the chapel, and stood before the tomb of Emilia Colonna. As he spoke he pointed to three words below the old inscription. To make room for them a bit of the ornamental border of the slab on which the name of Emilia was carved had been cut away. And as the old *custode* pointed at them with one hand, he shook his head again, with a look of commiseration, and tapped his forehead with the other hand once more.

But what he showed me·meant much to me. For there, beneath the name of Emilia Colonna, and the simple dates that told when she had come into the world and when she had left it, were the three words which in his last days the Cardinal Giulio had placed on her tomb,—

NVNC · IN · PACE

University Press : John Wilson & Son, Cambridge.

www.ingramcontent.com/pod-product-compliance
Lightning Source LLC
Chambersburg PA
CBHW030407270326
41926CB00009B/1306